Believe!

CHANGE YOUR MIND

10 UNCONVENTIONAL SECRETS TO RETRAIN YOUR BRAIN

WRITTEN AND LIVED BY COY WIRE

For Claire Francis,
Thank You for being my Source of strength through some of my toughest times, and my Source of happiness each and every day.
Always and all ways, I Love You.

For Rick & Jane Wire
I wouldn't be who I am today without You. Please know that I realize just how fortunate I am to have parents like You.

For Tiffany & Casey,
I will never forget that You have always been my biggest cheerleaders. I am humbled by Your Love and support. I am more thankful for You than I can possibly say.

For Grandma and Pappy, and all of my extended Family in Pennsylvania, California and Arizona...I Love You and I thank You for making me a better man. I dedicate this book to my Family. More than any other influence, I am who I am today because of You. I didn't write this book for You. I wrote it because of You.

I want to use this space to give thanks to my team of brilliant minds who helped this book manifest into a reality. Thanks to my genius editor Daniel Cox, my insanely creative designer and brand manager Joseph Szala, and one of my mentors, fellow Stanford Cardinal, Harry Beckwith. I am blessed to have been able to work with you. A special thanks goes to Jim Stump of Sports Challenge who initiated my Spiritual journey.

ISBN No. 978-0-9852929-0-4

Father,
Lead me to lead others.
Guide me to guide others.
Show me the Way to show
others the Way.

Amen.

CONTENTS

CHAPTER 5 - GOAL SETTING

CHAPTER 9 – ESSENTIAL STATES OF MIND

CHAPTER 10 – BECOME A BOOKWORM

CHAPTER 11 – TO BEE OR NOT TO BEE

Those who cannot change
their minds cannot change
anything

– George Bernard Shaw

INSPIRATION   PASSION   ACTION

CHANGE YOUR MIND • INTRODUCTION

Introduction

The contents of this book have been in the back of my mind since the age of 19. Extraordinary events in my life have been the impetus to put these contents onto paper. The pieces of this book have evolved from a handy compilation of lessons I learned from my predecessors, mentors and experiences to an unbelievable account of how I arrived at where I am today. Instead of merely telling my story, though, I have chosen to format some of what I have to share into keys of success that others can apply to their own lives.

Some of the magical insights that I discovered through conversation or experience were scribbled down on pieces of notebook paper, napkins or the back of my hand. One experience not only gave me a titanium plate and four screws in my neck, but also a valuable life lesson. Others were written down in the silence of my own room as a still small Voice within would speak to me. Some insights, however, were passed on to me from some of the greatest minds in history. Some of the greatest minds the world has ever known have spoken to me through books.

I once heard that there is one sentence in one book that will change your life forever. I understood that the purpose behind this thought was to get one to read, but after reading many books I realized that the phrase impacted my life in a very literal way. There have been single sentences in books that changed my entire perspective on life.

It has not only been books that have changed my life forever, however. There have also been many people, like angels, who have come down to give me messages that offer guidance and direction. Whether they come to us through books or other people, these messages are blessings. You may not know from whom, or how, or when, but at various points throughout your life you will be presented with profound insights that will be the impetus for great change in your life. They will be like magical, secret keys that you will be able to use to open great doors of opportunity in your life. The lesson behind this phrase is that we must seek those truths that we are meant to find.

My mother is the one who encouraged me to read books at a very young age. She told me that books could take me on magical journeys to places far, far away; and the best part was that I never even had to leave my bedroom to do so. I could meet famous people, even people who had passed away, by reading books. Mom was right. Books have changed my life for the better on many different occasions. I have tapped into the minds of some of the greatest philosophers throughout history. I have had tea with Bruce Lee discussing some of life's mysteries. Walter Payton taught me how to push my body to its limit. I was mentored by a 2,000-year-old wise man from a town called Bethlehem. I even received great life lessons from a jolly old fellow named Siddhartha. My first workouts and drills were taught to me by my dad who bought a book by Eric Dickerson. I still have that very same book. I received a valuable life lesson through a book that my sister, Tiffany, gave me. Believe it or not, I even met my SoulMate, Claire, because of a book my brother, Casey, gave me! I am humbled to find myself in a life that must be written about. I cannot stress enough that what I have experienced is incredible to the point of being absolutely surreal.

I wrote this book with intentions to inspire and guide you by sharing the insights that have inspired and guided me. My hope for this is that within these pages you may find one sentence that will change your life forever. Within these pages I have detailed 10 of the secret keys that have guided me towards success and happiness thus far on my journey here on this Earth. I pass on to you the lessons that have been passed on to me with the hope that you too can apply them to your life.

A Note Regarding God

This book is not about changing a person's beliefs. It's about helping anyone willing to change their mind and use their beliefs to accomplish great things. My aim is to encourage people to use what they already have. We are all more powerful than we know and we have God, whatever our individual definition of that is, in each of us.

It must be noted that, throughout the duration of this book, I will be referring to God. I was raised in the Christian faith. I am humbled by, and thankful for, my relationship and connection to God, but my intention is not to discourage those who do not personally connect with my God or any God for that matter. I realize that the Higher Power is referred to by many different names. God, Jesus, Buddha, Krishna, Jehovah, Mohammed, Adonai, Elohim, Yaweh, Elijah, Great Spirit and the I Am only begin to scratch the surface of how God is recognized around the world. To some, they are one in the same. For others, many may be obsolete. Either way, these are what I am referring to when I utilize the terms Power, Force, and God throughout the book. In many cases I capitalize words that may not traditionally be considered a proper

CHANGE YOUR MIND • A NOTE REGARDING GOD

noun. I do this because I see the divinity in all of God's creations and it's my way of showing honor to the Spirit within them.

I acknowledge and respect people who may have differing views about God. Who am I to say to whom you pray isn't right? I can only speak from my own personal experiences and humble understanding of God. I encourage you to translate my under-standing of God into whichever God-language you may speak. I hope that you try to listen past the specifics and hear the mes-sage behind them. When I speak of God, Spirit or Force, know that I am talking about that which is the greatest concept of one's self that one could possibly imagine. As long as you know that there is a Being, or part of yourself even, that is supreme to you, you will benefit from the message of this book.

Just because someone's concept of God may be different than mine, I'm not going to shut them out and not share with them all the wonderful messages God has shared with me. If the Medicine is good and the sickness is cured, it doesn't matter what we call It.

01

THE POWER
WITHIN

You Are What You ~~Eat~~ **Think**

I have always believed in a Higher Power. Even as a child watching Star Wars, there was something inside of me that believed in "the Force" and I thought I could learn how to use It. I wanted so badly to be a Jedi and be able to tap into that Power. I tried as hard as a young child could to acquire the Power. I would even sit for hours trying to make a cotton ball levitate using only the Power of my Mind. Yes, seriously. As I grew older, my curiosity about uncovering the Power also grew.

I asked all the eternal questions. What separated the mighty from the mundane? Why did it seem that there were only a select few who were able to achieve greatness?

I studied everything that I could about these titans with such Power. Eventually, I developed an affinity for imitating and emulating these people because I wanted to know their secrets. I concluded that after walking in their footsteps, it was only a matter of time before I stumbled upon their secrets. It didn't seem so far- fetched; after all, people like Plato, Socrates, Jesus, Lao Tzu,

Bruce Lee, Walter Payton and Einstein weren't all that different than me. The great ones were human just like me: two eyes, two ears, two hands, two feet, one brain and one heart beat. If they could be great, then I could too.

When I was nine years old I remember my dad talking to me prior to one of my wrestling matches. The opponent I was going to face was formidable, in the big, bad bully way and it was obvious that I was nervous. My Dad sat me down, looked me in the eye and said, "Coy, he puts his underwear on the same way you do".

That motto made me feel better and I have never forgotten it. It reminded me that the other guy didn't have any special abilities that I didn't have. Deep down, he probably had insecurities like I did. The only meaningful difference that would determine who would win was found in my mind and expressed through my attitude. My dad taught me how to get my Mind right. His pep talks made me believe I could win those matches. Because of that belief, I often did.

I grew to realize an understanding that changed my life

The great ones aren't different from everybody else.

They just THINK differently from everybody else.

People don't always believe what they see, but they always see what they believe.

forever: Those who are able to achieve greatness are those who are able to give themselves an edge mentally.

The things that separate those who are mighty from those who are mundane are their thoughts. I have seen this phenomenon firsthand during my nine seasons in the NFL. Battling on the same field as some of the best athletes in the world, I have observed that the most impressive players aren't necessarily bigger, faster or stronger. However, they BELIEVE they are. They convince themselves that they are destined to be great, and then their perception becomes reality.

There is a metaphysical thought that believing in specific things and focusing on them as positive thoughts will enable them to come true. The dominant theory is "like attracts like" and positive thinking results in positive actions coming to an individual.

I have realized that the great ones, whether they are athletes, doctors, musicians, philosophers, artists or entertainers, are those who are able to tap into an Almighty Power. They possess this Power in their very own Minds. Like them, you will become great and greater when you come to realize that we are what and how we think.

Absorb that right now: we are what we think. We are what we think. WE ARE WHAT WE THINK. All that we are, and all that we will become arises out of our thoughts. Our thoughts create our world.

In recent years there have been several books and movies released proclaiming that, with our thoughts, we can ATTRACT to ourselves anything that we desire. You may have heard it referred to as the Law of Attraction.

I understand what these books and movies are trying to say, but I feel that they are somewhat misleading. While many have benefitted from this philosophy, many others have been left dis- couraged, humiliated and heartbroken with dreams unfulfilled. When you say that you will ATTRACT into your life anything you want by thinking about it, it doesn't mean that you literally bring those things into your life. Putting it in this way makes it seem like magic.

I believe you don't ATTRACT the things you want in life, you NOTICE them!

We are a species with unfathomable amounts of ability and Power within. That Power has always been there. We are capable of so much more, physically, mentally and spiritually, than we are aware. Whether its greater self-confidence, improved health, more money or success, when you say that you can attract the things you want in life, it actually means that you evoke the Power within that enables you to TAKE YOURSELF TO THE THINGS YOU WANT, as opposed to them being brought to you.

The ability to have confidence, good health, better finances and success was always in you. Because of incorrect, or insufficient thinking, and lack of focus you were unable to envision the poss- Ability of making those things happen. The objects of your desires were always in your life, staring you right in the eyes, you just weren't able to see the opportunity to acquire them.

When you think correctly about the things you desire and properly focus on them you will see the opportunities to take them when they are present. When an opportunity that will help you get what you want presents itself, you will not miss it. You'll be waiting for it and, if you've prepared properly, you'll take advantage of the opportunity.

The mental and physical capabilities to get what you want out of life have always lived dormant within you. You've always been capable of having what you desire. When you focus your thinking, you summon all that is required from within to rise up and go get it.

It's not about the Law of Attraction. It's about the Laws of Action. Get up and go get it!

Others have also said that you can attract people into your life at the perfect moment, but you must know the truth. The truth is those people were going to come into your life at that time regardless of your thoughts. The only thing that changes is your mind and how you perceive that moment in time and space; what you are aware of in that moment. Your perception of the world around you and what you are able to perceive depends on the thoughts that are running through your mind in each moment.

Those people were going to be there, but did you notice them? Were too many incessant thoughts running through your mind that you did not even notice the person and you missed your opportunity? If you did notice them, were you in the right frame of Mind? Were you able to recognize the opportunity in encountering and interacting with them? Were you mentally prepared to meet that person and meet that situation positively?

This book is about the Laws of Action. It's about taking back control of your Mind and learning how to direct your thoughts. We must learn to control and direct our thoughts because they are what determine how we live and move in this world. When doors of opportunity open you must be prepared to run though them.

Our thoughts influence us. In fact, our thoughts influence everything. According to certain religious traditions, everything in existence was created by a single thought. A single thought created the heavens and the earth and everything in it. The Bible says, "In the beginning was the Word". Certain eastern religions say "Om" is the originating word or vibration that creates all things.

What is a word? A word is nothing more than a THOUGHT expressed verbally to communicate. Everything that has ever been created starts with a thought. Actions happen from the ideas in the mind that first appear as mental pictures.

Our thoughts shape our world. Our thoughts shape our growth and development. Our thoughts in each moment have a major influence on the type of day we will have. The types of days we have determine how our weeks will go. Those weeks become months, and those months become the years that make up our life. The type of life we will have is a direct result of the types of thoughts we have today. Think GOoD thoughts now so that you can look back someday and say that your life is filled with GOoDness.

I am thankful you have this book because that means many of the proper thinking tactics I have learned and used to enhance my life will be passed on to you. I am thankful that I am being given the opportunity to share my GOoD thoughts with you.

What are you thinking?

The Power Within

The Power within you is like God. It is the Light. It is Energy. It is the Spirit and Force flowing through us. In fact, this Power is not something that we need to find or tap into, because we already have access to It. We already use It every time we think! We just may not be aware that we are using It and how powerful each of our thoughts are. Ultimately, it is not a matter of locating the Power, but more about learning how to use the Power within properly.

Using it properly isn't easy and requires discerning choices. We must learn to control the Power so that we only give Power to the things we want to foster in our lives. Our Mind and its thoughts are what allow us to access this Power. Our thoughts, or our Mind, are not only the key to unlocking the door to this Power, but also the tools we use to harness and direct the Power.

The Power that is always flowing through us is like the Sun. The Sun radiates Power and Energy all the time and it does Powerful things to the Earth and all that's in it. It gives its Light and Energy to all it touches and sets into motion a myriad of happenings, every day. Although the Sun and its Power do much, it's capable of so much more. What it demonstrates on a daily basis

pales in comparison to its true capabilities. This is also true of our Minds.

Again, it is all a matter of learning how to use and hone the Power. If you take a magnifying glass and harness the same Energy given off by the Sun every day and focus the Power, It is magnified and becomes immensely stronger. Before the Sun would just warm and give Light to things on the Earth, but when focused, the same exact rays have the ability to Ignite.

Your thoughts can be the magnifying glass to harness and focus the Power and Light within you. Your Mind provides you the capability to focus your Energy on what you desire and Ignite those aspects of your life.

If we do not control our thoughts, the Power is subject to the randomness and chance of everyday life. We will end up giving Energy to frivolous things and neglecting significant Potential.

If you do not harness and hone the Power, nothing extraordinary will happen because you will only use a muted portion of the Power. You will make things happen and give Energy to things in your life, but nothing significant will happen until you focus that Energy. I'm not talking about a casual sort of focus either. In order to smash the status quo and become staggeringly good at what you do, you must employ a higher level of focus than those around you. Like my coach, Mike Smith, for whom I played at the Atlanta Falcons said, you must learn to "Zoom-Focus".

In order to avoid living a muted and diluted version of life, it is essential to harness and employ the Power with focused thinking. When the Power is focused, that is when magic happens. That is when we Ignite certain aspects of our life and become a man, or woman, on fire.

Find It

The main reason people are inhibited from utilizing and maximizing the Power is because they are looking for it in all the wrong places.

Many people search "out there" for the strength to get the things they desire. People think that what they want will come to them if they pray to the heavens, some skyward place, in hopes that God will hear them and grant them their wishes.

I have come to realize through my studies that the Force of God is not somewhere out there. It's quite the contrary: God is in You, Heaven is here.

After years of studying those able to accomplish incredible feats, as well as studying many different religions, I have come to the realization that the place where the Power that allows us to go from ordinary to extraordinary is within. Support for this is found in black and white in the Bible:

God wanted them to know that the riches
and glory of Christ are for you Gentiles, too.
And this is the secret: Christ lives in you.

-Colossians 1:27 (NLT)

The verse is evidence that points to the fact that you are more powerful than you know.

There is an Almighty Power within you. There are limitless treasures and storehouses of Energy and Intelligence within you. There is a sleeping giant inside of you waiting to be awakened and stirred from its slumber. There is a portal within you through which you can access this Higher Power. In fact, that Powerful Force stands at the doorway to your very own Mind and knocks, waiting for you to open the door and let It into your life.

Guess who has the key to this door: You. Guess what the key is made of: your thoughts.

Focus It

Another reason most people are not able to fully tap into the Power within is because most people today have very little or no real focus.

People spend too much time on too many irrelevant activities like Facebooking, Googling, gossiping, listening to stupid songs, playing video games or watching useless television programs. It's OK to do those types of things if you want to be a world-class video game player or a professional TV-viewer. If those are the things you want, then do them with a passion as often as you can, but if you have bigger and better dreams, then you need to focus your time and Energy on those bigger and better things. If you want to make serious progress in life, throw away your TV.

Sometimes, people just go through life wandering and thinking aimlessly, and the outcome of this unfocused life is shaped and molded by other people and external situations. Later in the book I talk about how humans conform to their surroundings. Without a focused, and guarded Mind, people are shaped by life, opposed to their shaping the life they want. Thought manifestation, or focused thinking, can change this. If you want to change your life, change your Mind.

Focused thinking will take you to the next level. No one achieves greatness by becoming a generalist. You don't hone a skill by diluting your attention to its development. The only way to get to the next level is to focus. No matter whether your goal is to increase your level of play, sharpen your business plan, improve your bottom line, develop your subordinates, or solve personal problems, you need to focus. Author Harry A. Overstreet observed, 'The immature mind hops from one thing to another; the mature mind seeks to follow through.'

-John C. Maxwell

In order to get the Power to work for us and bring our deepest desires to fruition, we must focus our Energy and Mind Power on activities that will bring us closer to what we seek. Like I mentioned earlier, our minds are like the Sun and with focused thoughts like rays through the magnifying glass, we can be more Powerful. That is what our Minds can do. If we do not focus our

Mind upon anything specific we never experience the full potential of the Power we possess.

In college one of my best friends, Simba, and I knew about and understood the Power of the Mind. We enjoyed testing the Mind and learning to use it more effectively. We came up with a game that would help us strengthen the Powers of the Mind. The game was simple; get people's attention using only our Minds.

Simba and I would go to a public place (most often a mall) and find a place to hang out that was out of the way and some-what discreet. We would locate a person who was far away and we would begin to focus our Minds on that person by repeating the phrase, "turn and look at me, turn and look at me, look at me, look at me". We chanted this over and over in our Minds, silently and pointedly until eventually the person would stop immediately whatever they were doing, pause and turn and look directly at us!

We got so good at it that we could do this without fail, every time. The best was when we would go up to the second floor of the mall and look down over the railing so that we could see people walking beneath us on the first floor. The reactions were price-less. We would spot our target, start chanting our prayer in our Minds and the person walking below would begin to walk slower, almost as if they were thinking of something. Then they would look to the left and to the right and suddenly they would stop and look up, directly at Simba and me. They would usually smile, we would smile back and then they would continue on their way.

One time, Simba and I were eating lunch outside with four other guys from the football team in the very busy student union at Stanford. We told our buddies about the ability we had developed and, of course, they laughed.

"Yeah right, whatever," they'd say. "You guys can't do that!" We said that we would prove it to them. We told them about the technique we used to get people's attention and asked that they join in on the process because we knew that it would be even more effective and Power-full if everyone focused their Minds together. We all agreed and determined that the next person to walk outside of the building would be the person we would focus our attention upon.

About 40 yards away a door opened and a guy carrying a snack emerged from the building. He was fiddling with his snack, and he started walking away from us so all we could see was his back. I told the group to focus and chant the prayer. As we intensely focused our Minds on the guy who was then about 50 yards away, he started walking very slowly, almost cautiously and he lifted his head. He took a few more steps and came to a complete stop. Simba and I knew what was about to happen. The guy, almost in a trance-like state, turned around and looked directly at our table! One of our friends, Travis Pfeifer shouted, "You've got to be kidding me!" The guy flashed us a big smile and then turned around and went on his way.

Needless to say, thought manifestation is real. I'm sure if you experiment with it yourself you'll have similar results. I feel that it is so powerful that it needs to be taught in schools to our children. It is a science as real as chemistry or physics. This type of study is probably more important and critical to our youth than any other field of study. Our schools must continue to teach our youth what to think, but kids also need to learn how to think.

Discovering the Power: My Awakening

You might be wondering if I have it in me to back up all of those strong statements about housing a mighty Force inside of you. I mentioned that I came to the "God is in You, Heaven is here" realization after doing a great deal of studying. This is true, but there was a specific event that ignited this insatiable need to get to the bottom of understanding such Power.

My true spiritual journey began during the winter quarter of my sophomore year at Stanford University. The winter quarter was always a fun time for the football guys, but this one was the best yet. We had just finished one of the greatest seasons that Stanford football had ever seen. We won the Pac-10 championship and made it to the prestigious Rose Bowl. Although we lost 19-7 to the high-powered Wisconsin Badgers, led by Heisman winner Ron Dayne, and standout receiver Chris Chambers, we were still on top of the world.

After the close of the season life became much more simple and relaxed. Our only obligations were to work out in the morning, go to class and make sure that we finished all of our school assignments on time. As long as we did those things, we could have fun, hang out and take full advantage of being a college student. And believe me; I was definitely taking advantage of all that college life had to offer! The frat parties and chill sessions with the fellas were amazing. I was truly enjoying my life and partying more than I ever had before.

One day while walking to the locker room at Arrillaga Family Sports Center to get ready for my weight room workout I was stopped by a short little stumpy fellow with a big shining smile on his face. He was older, maybe in his late 50's or so, and dressed respectfully. His head tilted to the side and with a twinkle in his eye, the barely five-foot tall man scurried up to me and said,

"Hi Coy! My name is Jim Stump!"

Before I could even grin about the irony of his name, he blurted, "Yes that's my real name. Stump! You can call me Stumper if you want."

This guy had incredible energy. He was so happy. I wondered how he knew me, and he explained that he was the team chaplain and said that he would love the opportunity to meet with me. I knew that the team chaplain was "the God guy"; the guy who would sit you down and preach to you about Jesus and all that religious stuff. Although I had grown up going to church every Sunday, and I did believe in God, I really didn't feel like hearing the whole gospel talk. Jim Stump and Sports Challenge guided thousands, but life was too much fun. I was enjoying being in college!

I politely brushed him off and said, "Yeah, maybe sometime that would be nice. I have to get going right now, though. I have to go work out. Maybe I'll see you around."

The kind little fellow said, "Ok great! See you around, Coy!"

I quickly walked off thinking to myself, "I hope I don't ever bump into him again because he seemed nice and I don't want to have to brush him off again."

Over the next few weeks, it seemed as if "Stumper" was stalking me. I knew he wasn't, but by "coincidence" I seemed to randomly bump into him almost every other day. Each time, he sported the same huge bright smile that radiated a friendly glow that was comforting to experience. Each time he reminded me that whenever I was ready he would love to sit and chat with me.

Eventually, there was something that came over me and said, "Coy, you should just sit and talk with the guy. He seems really nice and there's just something about him."

So, the next time I saw him, we set up a time to meet. I was actually kind of nervous about it. Was this guy going to grill me with all kinds of questions like:

"Are you happy with your life?"

"Have you been living up to your full potential?"

"Are you doing all the things you could be doing that will enable you to achieve your goals?"

Was he going to tell me that I needed to stop fooling around? Would he tell me that I needed to stop partying? Was he going to tell me that I needed to read the Bible and go to church all the time?

Those were some of the thoughts that were racing through my mind as I sat in the cafeteria of Arrillaga waiting for Jim Stump to meet me. Soon enough, Jim came strolling into the cafeteria, smiling as usual, saying hi to everyone he passed on his way to the table I had grabbed for us. I stood up and greeted him. As he looked in my eye, I felt an incredible sense of peace radiate from him that comforted me. Everything became still.

We started talking, and surprisingly, it wasn't preachy at all. He was just asking what I had been up to, how school was going and if I was enjoying the offseason. It was a great chat. It felt like I had known this guy forever, as if from another life.

As we finished our lunch, I couldn't help asking why he wanted to meet with me. He told me that he saw something special in me and that he felt it was part of his duty to meet with me. I couldn't help but think that this was part of the sales pitch and that he was going to start preaching. I thought this was the part where he was going to tell me to go to church and stop partying. To my surprise, he didn't do any of that. All he did was ask one simple question:

"Coy, do you want to be great?"

And as almost any college football player ready to conquer the world would answer, I replied "Absolutely, Mr. Stump."

"I thought so, Coy," he said. "Do you know how to do that" "Work hard?" I asked, raising my eyebrows, realizing I wasn't entirely sure.

Jim Stump smiled peacefully and said this:

"All you have to do is ask God to come into your life. Every night before you go to sleep and every morning as soon as you wake up, ask God to come into your life."

I was surprised and I asked, "So that's it?!? Just ask God to come into my life? I don't have to stop partying? I don't have to start going to church?!?"

"Nope," he said with a smile, "You don't have to change anything! You can indulge and party like any other college student and do whatever you want to do. None of that matters right now. Just ask God to come into your life."

So I did. Starting that night, I began to ask God to come into my life every night and every morning. And following Jim Stump's directions for greatness I didn't change anything else. What did I have to lose? I continued goofing around, having fun and going to parties. Not much changed in my life. I didn't notice anything different until one special night about three weeks later.

I was at a restaurant on University Ave. in downtown Palo Alto just hanging out with a few of my buddies from the football team. We were starting off the weekend with some grub and drinks before we headed back to campus to let loose at some of the parties that were going on that night. Then the conversation started to get interesting.

We started reminiscing about the football season that had just passed and the success we had. We talked about the upcoming season and how we could do even better things the next year.

The other thing that came up was the NFL. For everyone who was sitting at that table, making it to the NFL was the main aim. It was the reason we had chosen to go to Stanford. Along with the academics, choosing to play at Stanford provided the greatest opportunity for each of us to make it to the NFL, the lifelong dream for most of us. I had envisioned playing in the NFL ever since I was seven years old. It was my greatest hope and desire. It was all I had ever worked hard for.

My teammate, Tank Williams (who would eventually be a second-round draft pick for the Tennessee Titans) asked a question that ignited a spark within me and changed my life forever. He asked, "Hey Coy, when do the pro scouts come to Stanford to test us for Junior Pro Timing Day."

It was as if the whole world stopped in that instant. The room went silent, exactly like when you hold a seashell to your ear. I could hear silence. Time slowed down and the room got blurry and started to spin a little bit.

My mind was flooded with questions about myself and the life I had been living. Why was I not more focused? Why was I not working harder? Why was I wasting away my moments, moments that should have been used to better myself mentally and physically? All this time I had known what it is I want to do in life, yet I was wasting precious moments of my life searching for a good time.

In that one instant, because of that one question, I realized that the one thing for which I had always worked, making it to the NFL, was just around the corner. What had I been doing all this time? Why was I wasting so much time partying and goofing around? I didn't even realize the NFL scouts were going to come and see me

"A chief event of life is the day in which we have encountered a mind that startled us."

– Ralph Waldo Emerson

work out in a few short months!

These overwhelming realizations and feelings continued to gush in. As if in a trance, I stood up, turned to the door and walked out of the restaurant. I didn't say one word to any of the people I was with nor did I bother finish eating or drinking or even paying for my dinner. I just walked right across the street and got into my car.

As I sat down I felt this incredible Energy begin to flow through my body, like I had been attached to a generator and electricity was flowing through my veins. This incredible Force that began flowing freely through my body was amazing. I sat and stared out the windshield of my car and knew undoubtedly what was happening to me. I remembered Jim Stump. I remembered what I had been asking every day for the past three weeks. And then a voice spoke to me. In a whisper it said:

"God is in You, Heaven is here."

I remember getting back to my room that night and I did something I'd never done while in college. At 9:30 on a Friday night, I knelt down at the side of my bed and began to cry. They were not tears of sadness, though. They were tears of complete joy. I was so happy that I was crying. I was so thankful that I had been given the gift of realizing the universe's greatest secret. The Voice within me whispered the secret once again:

"God is in You, Heaven is here."

As I stayed there on my knees at bedside with my head in my hands, a wealth of realizations rushed in. All of the unique experiences and situations that I had experienced up until that point in my life were trying to get me to this realization all along. Everything made sense.

I knew in that instant that anything I wanted to do, no matter how great or grand, I could do. Even the thing that seemed the most difficult of all, making it to the NFL, was within my reach. I was thankful for the realization that I was going to make it to the NFL. In that instant, I knew the only thing stopping me was me.

Like being shot from a canon, I went from living life mostly unconscious and unaware of what I was doing to myself with my own thoughts and actions to the magical world of Consciousness and Awareness. I had experienced an awakening. It was a monumental moment in my life.

I woke up from living a monotonous and boring life; a life in which I seemingly had no real control. It was a life that just, as they say, happened the way that it was supposed to happen. I realized that my life was not the victim of the chaos theory; my life was not the result of a series of random events over which I had no control. I had been in control the whole time. I was just not choosing the things I should have been choosing. I was experiencing in my life the exact results that came from the way I was thinking. I woke up and saw with my own eyes, for the first time, the reality of the world in which I was living. I realized that life was not random and out of my control. I realized that I was living the exact life that I had been creating for myself!

And in that awakening moment I also realized that the life I was going to experience in the future would be of my own creation.

I had been en-Lightened. The Light came in and illuminated my world so I could see clearly the reality of the life I was living. I was enlightened to the realization that I was the captain of my ship. No longer would I have to live in the dark. I once had been blind, but now I could see. I finally realized that I was the one who, through a series of my own choices and decisions, had created the very life that I was experiencing.

That night, in the stillness of my room, my Spirit, Soul or Consciousness floated up out of my body. I had an out of body experience. My Spirit (the real me) rose up out of my physical body like incense and actually hovered above my physical body. I looked down at my physical body kneeling down beside the bed and realized that it was just a vessel. The physical body was just a compilation of everything inside me: skin, muscles, bones, capillaries and atoms. It was completely obedient to the Thinker within, the Captain of the ship. I realized that no matter what I, the spiritual entity, wanted my body to do or think is exactly what would happen.

I realized that I had spent entirely too much of my life doing nothing, or at the very least, not enough! I had now come to the realization that I could do anything and I mean the liberal anything that includes anything you can imagine.

Anything I had done up until that very moment was a decision that I had made. Even the things I hadn't done, the things I could've or should've done, didn't happen because of the decisions I had made. The things that didn't happen in my life did not happen because I didn't make them happen.

There was no excuse. It wasn't because of someone else holding me back or because I wasn't physically able. I was not the victim of any circumstance or situation. Everything that did, or did not, happen in my life was because of me and no one else.

Dr. Hawkins is world-renowned psychiatrist, physician, researcher and pioneer of consciousness and spirituality research.

My experience is best described by Dr. David Hawkins when he described what seems to be the same type of awakening I experienced:

"Suddenly, the Bhagavad Gita made complete sense; eventually the same spiritual ecstasy reported by Sri Ramakrishna and the Christian saints occurred. Everything and everyone in the world was luminous and exquisitely beautiful. All living things became radiant, and expressed this radiance in stillness and splendor. It was apparent that all of mankind is actually motivated by inner love, but has simply become

CHANGE YOUR MIND • THE POWER WITHIN

unaware; most people live their lives as though they're sleepers unawakened to the perception of who they really are."

Over the next few months I was invincible. I had incredible Energy. I felt a Light shining through me and I knew that others felt it too. Extreme love and happiness had swept over my entire being and I felt it in every movement and moment of my days. Just like the subject of the magnifying rays, I had become ignited and was a man on fire. Nothing was impossible to me.

The way this Spirit flowed through and affected my physical body was amazing. I had ceaseless Energy. One day during our off-season conditioning program some Stanford scientists came to test out a new type of technology on the players.

The device they used was a little glass tube, big enough to put your hand and forearm in it. There was a vacuum seal that closed off the outside air to your hand and forearm. Inside the tube was a handle of ice-cold metal coils.

The purpose of the device was to lower your body temperature so that you could run longer and faster without getting as tired. The vacuum would bring the blood running through your hand and arm to the surface of your skin, and when the blood passed through your hand that was holding the metal coils, your blood would be cooled. When this cooled blood travelled back to your heart it would prevent the body from overheating during exercise and prevent you from getting tired. The user could run faster, farther and longer than someone who was not using the device.

I chose not to be one of the test rats, so I ran the conditioning without the fancy gadget. I didn't need it. I had my own device that gave me super powers and it resided within me. This particular day we were running 300's and if you've ever run 300's for conditioning you know that it's punishing. If you haven't run them, they are hellish sets of sprints that evoke trials of subsequent vomiting. The scientists timed everyone, those with device and those without it, so that they could prove how the athletes who did not use the device would get more tired as the session continued. The theory was that their times would get slower and slower with each 300 that was run.

I ran and I ran. I ran like a champion, reciting a mantra and prayer in my head with every set I ran. When we finished the last 300 for the day, the head scientist walked over to me with a dumbfounded expression on his face.

He said, "Son, may I ask you a question?"

"Sure", I replied with a smile on my face in anticipation of what he was about to ask.

"What are you doing," he asked with a very concerned look on his face.

"What do you mean, sir?"

"We are here doing an experiment, and we found that the athletes who were using this device were able to endure the 300's better than those who did not. Although their times were slower with every 300 they ran, their times did not drop as much all those who did not use the device, all except for one. That one was you. We found that instead of your times getting slower with each 300 you ran, your times got faster! When you were supposed to be getting tired and running slower times, you got stronger. How do you do that?"

Without any hesitation I gave him an answer that most scientists would not want to hear.

"It's the Spirit," I said. "It's God, sir. It's the Spirit flowing through my body that enables me to do these things."

Aside from having ceaseless Energy I experienced many other extraordinary gifts. I was clairvoyant. In one instance I got a vision in my Mind that a friend I hadn't spoken to in quite a while was in pain. Sure enough, I called him and he said that someone in his family had died and that he was so glad that I had called because he really needed someone to talk to.

In another instance I was in the car with friends driving to San Francisco, and the person driving realized they didn't know how to get to where we wanted to go. Nobody else in the car knew either, but suddenly I just knew how to get there. Though I'd never been there before, the way just came to me. My friend was just getting ready to pull over to ask someone how to get there and I shouted, "Stop, I know how to get there!" Turn after turn, I gave the directions to the location through the labyrinth-like city with precision and accuracy.

All of these moments were exceptional and I always embraced them as small miracles, blessing my life and allowing me to be exactly who I was trying to become.

A New Outlook

I've been fortunate to experience many magical moments. Throughout each one, I felt an undercurrent of extreme peace flowing through me that I never knew existed. It was a certain Peace that came from knowing and realizing that I was the Master of my own fate. In that moment in the restaurant at Stanford that night, I had experienced the great "I Am". I studied the philosopher Descartes during my freshman year at Stanford, and his famous creed always stuck with me: "I think therefore I am."

René Descartes was a 17th-century French philosopher, mathematician and writer. He is considered the "Father of Modern Philosophy" and much of Western philosophy is a response to his studies and writings.

Although I understood what the phrase meant to him, I came to find a slightly different meaning. For me, "I think therefore I am" was actually a fill in the blank.

I think, therefore I am _____ or I think, therefore I am (whatever I think I am).

Whatever I think I am, I actually am, or can be. Whatever I think I am not, I simply am not. Siddharta Gautama knew this. That is why he said:

The mind is everything. What you think, you become. All that we are is the result of what we have thought. If a man speaks or acts with an evil thought, pain follows him. If a man speaks or acts with a pure thought, happiness follows him, like a shadow that never leaves him.

If I had thoughts of partying and goofing around while I was at college, then that's what I would get. If I focused my thoughts on becoming a professional football player in the NFL, then that's the direction my life would go. If I spent my thought-life on both party-ing AND making it to the NFL, then I'd probably end up getting something in between. Like the old adage says, "you can't serve two masters". If you do, you will never fully experience either of them. You will only get a little taste of what each has to offer.

I realized that whatever I focused my attention and thoughts on most, is what would manifest in my life. In other words, be-cause I can think, I will become whatever I think I will become. I had come to the realization that there was a mighty Power flowing through me. This Power had always been there, but I hadn't realized it. It was like an untapped and untamed Force that was sleeping inside of me.

It was right there for me all along but I had never grasped the concept completely and I never truly understood how Powerful each of us can be. Nobody had ever told me exactly how to access this Power and utilize it. Thank GOoDness I was shown a Way to experience this Power within.

The world as I had always known it had disappeared. I was now living in a new world with new poss-Abilities. This new shimmery world was a beautiful place. It was almost as if I was living and walking in Heaven right here on Earth. I could feel an amazing Energy and Spirit flowing in and through me. It was the Energy and Spirit of God.

Now I saw a new heaven and a new earth, for the first heaven and the first earth had passed away.

-Revelations 21:1

KNOW
THYSELF

Temet Nosce

You Are Not Your Past

Had I not had that enlightening experience that night in my bedroom, I would never have realized that I was a prisoner of my own Mind. I would never have realized that my development was arrested. That awakening experience allowed me to come to the realization that I needed to change my Mind. I needed to liberate myself from the confines of misguided and misdirected thought so that I would be free to become the best that I could possibly be. That awakening allowed me to see who I really was and what I was truly capable of.

Do you know who you are? Do you know what you are capable of? You have had choices in your life and you have made decisions. What type of person have you created yourself to be in this very moment because of those decisions? When you look in the mirror are you happy with the results of your decisions looking back at you?

Maybe you could have worked harder, sacrificed more, treated people better and made wiser decisions. If this is the case, that's ok. Although you may have been using the Power carelessly, the

COY WIRE • WWW.COYWIRE.COM

beauty of this Power is that it is limitless. You can always access it and use it to create Positive change in your life. You can literally recreate your entire life and change it for the better, right now. You can change your Mind.

At this juncture in your life, who are you? Most people, when asked that tell you who they WERE. When asked that question, most people instantly think about things they have done in the past to describe who they are in this moment. They think about past accomplishments and accolades. They reminisce about past relationships. They refer to past victories or failures, but what you have done in the past is not who you are. It is only who you were at one time.

The things of your past were done by a different person than the one who is reading this book right now. You have grown and developed into a new being because of the experiences you have had. You are more wise and crafty than you once were. Hopefully, you are more erudite, resilient and mentally tougher than you were in the past.

Many make the mistake of living in the past and dwelling in a time that no longer exists. Everything that has happened in our past is a figment of our imagination. It doesn't actually exist any-more other than as a memory. Things in our past can only affect us if we allow them to.

Whether our past was good or bad, we often rely too heavily upon it and it affects the way we act in the present moment, which is the only thing that is actually real. We must never allow our past to influence our thoughts and actions in the present moment. Sure, we can learn from our past and use it to help us make wiser decisions, but we must not allow it to prevent us from treating the present moment as the completely unique and original gift that it is.

Living a life too heavily influenced by your past imprisons you and builds up walls that trap you and prevent you from seeing all the opportunities that lay in the present moment.

The past is like a finger pointing away to the moon.

Don't concentrate on the finger or you will miss all that heavenly glory.

-Bruce Lee

If the moon is our destiny, our full potential in the present moment, then we must not be distracted by our past. We use our past to help guide us and point us in the right direction, but we mustn't be blinded by it.

The things you have done in the past, whether good or bad, do not define you.

Eventually, people get to a certain point in their lives and, based on the life experiences they have had up until that point, feel that that is who they are and they cease to progress.

They begin to say, "I'll never have this" or "I'll never be able to do that". They pinpoint the type of person they think they always will be and accept it.

They may see a more successful or happier person than themselves and, because of past experiences, they say, "I will never be like that."

It is exactly this type of negative self-talk that cripples people. When you get to the point where you start saying things like that, you're done. You may have been hope-full at one time, but at this point you are hope-less, if not hope-none. You never give yourself the chance to be any better than you already are if you dwell in your past.

You are capable of doing so much more with your life than you realize. I want you to read that sentence again.

You can do so much more, be so much more and go so many more places with your life than you realize. You must constantly free yourself from your past so that it can never get its grips on you.

Think of your past as quicksand along a path. It always wants to suck you in and hold you back. The longer you dwell there the more stuck you get. The past is also like a living entity, a monster even, that wants to trap you and keep you with it so that you can't progress any farther on your journey. When you free yourself from your past, you can continue to progress. When you realize that you are not your past, the world of possibilities opens up again. You are free to be all that you are meant to be.

Free yourself from your past so that you can see who you are, of what you are capable and where you can go. Who are you now? Where are you going now? What kind of life are you creating for yourself right now?

We are not what we have done in our pasts. We are who we are, right now, in this moment of time and space.

Who you will be in the future depends on what you do today. Wipe the slate clean and begin to create for yourself the life you desire.

Forget about all those missed opportunities because there will be new ones. Forget about the girl, or guy, that got away because there is another who cannot wait to meet you. Forget about the times you let your friends down because you can choose now to be the best friend they have ever had. Forget about the times you lied so you can choose now to speak the truth always and in all ways. Forget about all the times you showed up late because now you can set your alarm earlier. Forget about all the bad food you have eaten; you can eat healthier from here on out. Forget about your past. From this moment on you are free from your past. You have repented from the mistakes you have made and you can choose to live a life full of love, passion and integrity.

There is No One in the World Like You

To thine own self be true

–Shakespeare

What do you want to do with your time here on this earth? If someone were to ask you that, would you be able to answer it with certainty and conviction? I have found that many people cannot. People may know some of the broad and general things they'd like to accomplish, but most people aren't able to give specifics when they are asked what they

"Know thyself" is an Ancient Greek aphorism attributed to many Greek philosophers, including Socrates. It's generally regarded as a statement about individuality and the idea that the opinion of others should have little bearing on the opinion of yourself.

want to do with their time here on Earth. That question is synonymous with the Socratic theorem, "Know thyself".

Do you really know who you are? Do you know what you really want? Do you know what you are capable of? If you don't know what you want, and if you don't know who you are, how will you ever be what you are meant to be? It is critical to understand yourself, to know of what you are capable and what your true purpose is in life.

Being able to answer the question of what you want in life is powerful. It is not an easy question to answer if you have not studied your Self. One of my favorite parts of my MindTraining sessions with my clients is when I ask them what they WANT to do with their life.

"Well, I think I want to be a doctor; I think a heart doctor," they might say.

"I think I want to be the top sales person in my company," someone else might say.

From the way that they answer the question, I am able to hear doubt and hesitation. I am able to hear that they aren't quite sure what they want to do with their lives. They think they know, but they do not know with no uncertainty.

After that exercise, I ask them what they WILL DO with their life.

They look at me with a startled look in their eyes and they realize that it isn't about what we MIGHT DO with our lives, but it is instead a matter of what we WILL DO with our lives.

The difference in the way that question is asked is profound. It forces us to realize that this life of ours is ours, and that we will do with it whatever we choose.

Each of us have been uniquely created with our own gifts and missions and we must go deep within our own hearts to know what it is we were sent here to do on this Earth. When you know what you want to do with your life you have begun to understand who you really are.

Robert Collier was a 20th century self-help author of books discussing the psychology of faith, confidence and achieving your best. Late in his life he began writing about the use of the mind to achieve success in all walks of life.

We each have a purpose and were sent to complete a mission, which only we can perform, that benefits the greater good. As Collier says, "the various forms of plant life, of animals, of man - all are mere cogs in the great scheme of things."

As the hands of time tick away, each of us is a cog wheel spinning, serving its purpose and setting into motion energy that empowers another cog to keep the whole thing moving. We are all connected and each of us is vital and pertinent. We each have a purpose. Each of us is a Child Of God (C.O.G.), with a purpose in the mechanism and workings of Life.

There is no one in the world like you, absolutely no one. You are completely unique and original. There may be others out there with qualities and characteristics that are similar to those you possess. Some people out there probably have the same type of hair or eyes that you have. There may be some people who look a little bit like you. Surely there are people out there who walk like you or talk like you. There may even be someone out there who looks almost exactly like you, but I can assure you that there is nobody on this Earth exactly like you.

When you come to understand that there is nobody else in the world like you, you begin to realize that you are special. You will begin to realize that everything about you, even the seemingly bad qualities, is what makes you special and unique. If people would just accept themselves for who they are and for how they are, they would be much happier. Other people would enjoy being around them more too. They would be like a superstar or an enigma; someone that nobody has ever seen before.

In your mind, envision someone you think is cool, really cool. Maybe it is a movie star like Scarlett Johannson or Johnny Depp. Maybe a singer like Lady Gaga or a hip hop mogul like Jay-Z. Maybe it's an artist, or somebody from school or the person at work that is known by everyone to be the coolest, smoothest around.

What makes this person so special and unique?

You will probably find that the reason this person is intriguing is simply because they are different. There is nobody else quite like them. You know why that is? It's because they are content being themselves. They don't try to be someone that they are not. They dress the way they want to dress, talk the way they want to talk and move the way they want to move. Yes, they have problems too and they're not perfect. However, they don't care because that's just who they are. They are who they are because they do things in their own unique way. This quality comes across to others as being very appealing and intriguing.

These people are comfortable and confident in almost any situation. They never seem to be flustered or frazzled. They always seem to be cool, calm and collected in their very own way. This is because they are not worried about what other people think. They are quite content with who they are and, no matter what the situation, they seem to have an air of confidence. This confidence is the type of confidence that can only come from the deep sense of peace that they have within themselves. This deep sense of peace can only come from knowing who you are, accepting who you are and liking who you are. Most very cool people are at peace with themselves.

A vast majority of the people in our world are not comfortable with who they are. They are not at peace with themselves. Because they are not comfortable with who they are, and because they are not at peace with themselves, these people try to change who they are so they can be like somebody else.

This is the worst mistake anyone can make and it's unfortunate that most people live their entire lives unhappy because they make this mistake. If someone is not happy with who they are they begin to look to other people to emulate. If they don't like themselves, they look to another person who they consider cool and try to be like them.

T.D. Jakes is a Dallas, Texas pastor of a non-denominational church of over 30,000 members. He has written numerous works and has produced countless televised church and evangelistic services. He has been a spiritual advisor to the past two Presidents of the United States.

When a person is unhappy with who they are and they try to be like someone else, they lose themselves. They lose everything that makes them unique and special. They lose the uniqueness that gives them the ability to be that cool, confident person they were striving to be. They could have been cool all along. They had "it" all along, they just didn't realize it. In trying to be like someone else, they have become what T.D. Jakes described as a "cheap copy of a great original".

When you try to be someone you are not, you come across as fake. You become just like one of those plastic fruits that kind of looks the part but everyone knows is not real. Or, you become just like those ugly fake plants with the silk fabric flowers in the corner of your living room while everyone wonders why you didn't just buy a real plant. You kind of resemble the look you're going for but you pretty much look just plain stupid.

Each of us is a great original. When we are ourselves and we aren't trying to be someone else or something we are not, we are really great! There is no one in the world like us when we are content to be who we are. But as soon as we start talking and acting like others, we become a cookie cutter, main stream or a "seen that type of person before" type of individual.

If you decided you didn't like the person you are and that you were going to try to be like Madonna or Brad Pitt, you would be making a huge mistake. You would try to walk and talk and dress like them but you would come across as a being disingenuous. People would look at you and say, "Look at that guy, he thinks he's Brad Pitt."

Be you-tiful and be happy.

Evaluate Your Self:
Who are you?

The unexamined life is not worth living

— Socrates

One of the greatest keys to getting what you want in life is setting goals. Later in the book we will talk about the secrets of setting goals. First, however, it is crucial to realize who you are because if you don't know who you are you will not be able to set realistic and logical goals.

If you don't set realistic goals you will not be able to become all that you are meant to be and you will waste a lot of time building a life that wasn't meant for you. If an eagle was to spend its entire life hanging around chickens, walking and clucking as one and thinking that it's only a chicken, it would never experience all the glory and splendor that represents an eagle.

Don't get me wrong, chickens are great, but you can't spend your entire life being a chicken. Some of the most profound statements and words of wisdom come from young kids. Remember when you were in kindergarten and little Johnny shouted, "Stop being a chicken and go for it!" Johnny was right.

Before you can ever stop being a chicken, you must first realize that you are not one! You must Know Thyself and realize how powerful you really are. You must Know Thyself better than any other thing that you know; all of your strengths and the supposed weaknesses. When you Know Thyself you will be able to begin to set goals that are in alignment with what is meant for your life. You begin to know what you really want and you will be able to set realistic goals that help propel you toward the glorious destiny you were meant to achieve. You will be an Eagle. You will fly high and enjoy a long life and a lofty view.

To ensure your direction
Perform Self-reflection

How do you find out who you really are so that you can set realistic goals for your life? You must practice self reflection. This is one of the most important and vital keys that I can give you. It is a secret that many successful people have used over the years. Mages, sages, kings, queens, artists, inventors, authors and musicians have meditated on every aspect of their life. Even Jesus himself "went off to the mountains by himself to pray and meditate."

MED·I·TATE
verb
med·i·tat·ed med·i·tat·ing
Definition of MEDITATE
intransitive verb

1: to engage in contemplation or reflection

2: to engage in mental exercise (as concentration on one's breathing or repetition of a mantra) for the purpose of reaching a heightened level of spiritual awareness

transitive verb

1: to focus one's thoughts on : reflect on or ponder over

2: to plan or project in the mind : intend, purpose

This secret technique has helped me immensely over the years. I firmly believe that if we are ever going to be all that we are meant to be, we must truly know who we are and all of which we are capable. We must know ourSelves. With today's fast paced society in which we live it's near impossible to have a still mind to see and know ourSelves.

With all of the visual and audible distractions on TV and radio, with all of the parties, social gatherings, work, school, appointments, meetings, activities and functions our minds become so bogged down during the course of a day that we never have a single quiet moment for ourselves to simply sit and be still. When was the last time you spent time with yourSelf? When is the last time you had a deep heart to heart with yourSelf? Have you taken time to hear what You have to say?

We never have time to sit and think about who we are, what we want and what we like or don't like. We often have no choice but to think about everything that is going on around us. It's always about other people around us. We are so inundated mentally and emotionally that we are rarely able to unplug from the madness to sit back and say "Ahhhh, there You are, Self. How have You been? What have You been up to? I haven't seen You in so long."

Most of us don't even remember what we look and sound like.

In order for us to be at one with ourselves and know who we are we must take time each day to step away from the commotion and madness of our hectic world and just be still. To connect with yourself, you must meditate. This is how I do it.

Twice each day I go to my room or a quiet place. I close the door and turn off the lights and I sit in the silence. As I consume the silence, every inch of my body relaxes, from my feet to my ankles and into my hips and through my abdomen. The relax- ation continues on to my chest and shoulders, through my arms, elbows, wrists and fingers. It ends with my neck and face and to the top of my head. Once I'm in a near-unconscious state of mind I begin to focus on my breath. I listen to my breath and feel it as the air goes in and out of my body. I imagine a windmill in my wind- pipe, its sails spinning in constant fashion. Air circulates through my lungs but there is no beginning and end, keeping the windmill spinning constantly. I calm my body and my mind and sort through the waves of agitation in mind. Then I consider the Thinker within, recognizing and acknowledging the Consciousness that controls my thinking and decision making.

I then separate the Consciousness from my physical body. I cause the Consciousness to float up out of my body and I imagine It coursing through my body and out the top like sweet smoke circling skyward. My Spirit floats above my physical body seated below. Looking down at my physical body, I see it as just flesh, a collection of water, bone, protons, electrons and neutrons, clothed in skin. As I look down I realize my body is completely subject to the Will within. My Consciousness is the decision maker for me, my Master Mind, the force behind the system of blood and bone that sits below. If I tell my hand to rise, it will. If my Consciousness tells the body below to speak, the words of my Consciousness will be spoken. If I tell the body to be silent and still, it will.

When you float above your own physical body you are able to see what you have been doing with your life. What have you been telling your body to do? Are you doing all the things you should be doing or are you doing those things you know you should not? Are you making strides towards being the person you wish to be or is your life more like running on a treadmill, constant action but getting nowhere? Are your thoughts, words and deeds reflections of the person you wish to be? Are you making wise decisions? Are you choosing wisely the people with whom you surround your-Self? Are you taking full advantage of the moments you've been given here on this Earth?

It's humbling to know that you have the Power within to create the life you choose for yourSelf and the body that sits below. It's humbling to think that you are the Master of the fate of the vessel that sits below. Whatever you tell it to do, it will do.

Just sit there as you float and hover, reflecting on the choices you've had and the decisions you've made. Think about your past thoughts, actions and words. Think about the direction you want that body to move the moment you go back into it. Create a plan for yourSelf. Take back the Power and control of the body. Don't let the fleshly body, the busy brain and other outside physical forces control and influence you.

After hovering for about five minutes, I envision that Smoke and that Essence which is swirling above and I begin to imagine It making Its way back down into the body below.

I envision It creeping back in through the top of the head and back into the body. I feel It seeping back into the brain and I feel It press against the back of the eyelids that are closed. I feel the Essence go through the mouth and throat and back into the chest, filling the shoulders then moving down the arms, wrists and hands. I feel the Presence regain form in the abdomen, hips, legs knees, ankles, feet and toes. When the Spirit has returned completely to Its temporary home in your body, you are now fully present again in your physical body. You have completely returned to the physical realm.

You then slowly think back to your breath and you feel the air going in and out of your physical body. You should feel a sense of power, strength and ability to do anything. You should feel a heightened awareness of all that is you. You are back in control and now you make the calls. As the captain of your Soul, you steer the ship. Then you slowly open your eyes. Look out world, here I come!

At least twice a day, float up out of your body and meditate. Perform Self-evaluation and analysis each time. Take time to sit and be still, float up out of your body and look down upon it. What are you doing? Are you doing all of the things you should be doing? Are you making strides towards being the person you wish to be? Are your thoughts, words and deeds reflective of the type of person you wish to be?

And in the morning, rising up a great while before day, he went out, and departed into a solitary place, and there prayed.

–Mark 1:35 KJV

And when he had sent the multitudes away, he went up into a mountain apart to pray and when the evening was come, he was there alone.

-Matthew 14:23 KJV

But Jesus often withdrew to lonely places and prayed.

-Luke 5:16 NIV

Wake Up!!!

Whether you know it or not, you have already been using the Power.

One thing that you must come to learn, understand and BELIEVE is that you hold the key to your future. You must take complete responsibility for your actions and be able to live your life as if the following phrase is a universal truth: I am the master of my own fate.

Look at the person in the mirror and realize that the person you see before you is who he or she is because of all the choices you have made in life up until that very moment. Every decision you have made in your life has brought you to become the person you see before you. From the clothes you are wearing to the types of food you have eaten, your present life circumstances are a direct result of the decisions you have made.

Who you are is not by mere chance, some random series of fortunate or unfortunate events, nor were you the victim of circumstances. You are who you are because of the decisions you have made. You are reading this book right now because a series of small choices has led you to this very moment in time and space. What you do after you stop reading this book will be determined by a decision YOU make.

It's time for you to wake up and realize that you've been living your life mostly on auto-pilot. You've been going through the motions, making a few pointed decisions here and there, but for the most part you've just been going with the flow. You've been letting life happen to you as opposed to you making life happen the way you want it to.

We often see this after a person goes through some major disappointment, failure, catastrophe or even a near-death experience. After such events the person achieves success or somehow turns their life around for the better. Why does it take a tragedy, illness or "wake-up" call for some of us to turn our lives around? What happens during a near-death experience? In the moments that a person's life comes crashing down around them, during the time that they see their world falling apart, they have an awakening. They realize that it was all of the things they did or did not do that have brought them to that point in their life. Their entire life flashes before their eyes.

A near-death experience allows a person to take a look back at the life they have lived up to that point and enables the person to see that they were in total control of the vehicle or body until that point. They were the captain of the ship all along. They were the one choosing towards which destination the vessel was headed. When their entire life flashed before their eyes, they realized that all of the things they had done and all of the places they had been was a result of the decisions they had made in their life.

They realize that if they were to survive, where they would go from that point on, and what they would say and do, would be up to them too. The experience made them aware of the Power that was within them. They realize that they have always had access to it.

Be mindful of the life you are living. Where are you steering your ship? What destinations are you choosing for yourself? What types of thoughts are you having? What types of decisions are you making? Are you asleep at the wheel? Many of us are near death, but have years and years ahead of us.

Create a great life for yourself by stacking up one great decision after another.

Neo is a fictional character from the film "The Matrix", who unlocks numerous powers and abilities when he disconnects from the Matrix, a force controlling everyone in a virtual reality.

Wake up and stop sleepwalking through life. Stop falling asleep behind the wheel and take control of your vessel and steer it. Don't wait until something traumatic happens in your life before you become aware of the Power that is within you. Don't let a missed opportunity be your wake up call. Don't let the direction of your life be determined by the randomness and haphazardness of life. Do not be manipulated any longer by the world around you going whichever way the wind blows. Stop letting what other people say and do influence you so much. Stop letting magazines and television influence your decisions so much. Stop letting pop culture and mainstream society determine what you think is important and how you dress, the way you talk and the type of people you hang with. Just like Neo in "The Matrix", you need to be unplugged from the system so that you can wake up and see how this world really works.

Startle yourself! Give yourself an awakening or a "chief day", as Emerson would say, and startle your mind so that it wakes up! Wake yourself up so that you can see the world around you for what it really is before it's too late and most of your life has passed you by.

Think of your life as a movie that has been playing ever since you were born. You are the star, the writer and the director at the same time. In your mind, you have determined how the script would go and then you went along and acted it out. Some scenes were happy scenes. Some were sad. Some scenes were messy. Some were sexy. Some scenes were... well, you get the point. Wake up and realize that who you are now is a result of all that has gone on in your mind.

The 19th-century American essayist and poet, Ralph Waldo Emerson led the Transcendentalist movement. On awakening, he said this: "A chief event of life is the day in which we have encountered a mind that has startled us."

You are not who you are because of the world around you. The world around you is how it is because of YOU.

When you realize that all you have become up until this moment in your life has been the result of all the decisions YOU have made in your life, you then come to a very powerful realization: whatever you will become in the future will be a direct result of the decisions you make.

Every thought you have and decision you make from this very moment forward will affect your destiny.

In regards to our own thoughts and decisions, the law is simple. Every little seemingly insignificant thought that you will have

and every little decision that you will make will determine your future. This is a law of the universe that is as real as the law of gravity, what goes up must come down. What goes out must come back in. Whatever thoughts we allow out will come back again.

What goes on up in your head in the heavenly places will manifest down here in the earthly realm.

Startle yourself! Shake yourself, pinch yourself and wake up! Realize how this world works and how your mind works. You literally have the power to change the world in which you live. It all starts with a single thought or vision.

See, in your mind, the changes you would like to make in your life. Once you have that vision clearly in mind, you've already won more than half the battle. When you know exactly what you want you will then be able to come up with a plan to make that vision manifest in the world around you. You will be like a great magician with the power to make anything you wish appear in your life. If you want to make your world a better place you can! Like Gandhi said, "Be the change you wish to see in the world"

If you want your life to change; change your mind.

Born to Succeed

You are a direct descendent of the greatest kings and queens who have ever walked the Earth. There is Greatness within you.

Did you know that you were born to succeed? All of us have already overcome incredible odds. We are all winners. We have within us what it takes to succeed. I wrote this one day while considering that all of us come from greatness:

> When I was younger, my parents put me in a race...a swimming race. There were thousands of other youngsters in the race. I remember it like it was yesterday. We were all lined up, ready and anxious, with tensions rising. It was getting heated and intense and then...Bang! The gun went off. We all just started to swim. It was crowded, jam-packed as we swam. I got bumped, bruised; it seemed almost like some sort of torture at moments. I wasn't sure why my parents put me in this race. I swam and swam, kicked and pulled. I didn't really know

why I tried so hard, I just did. With everything I had I swam and I swam. I wanted to win. I believed I was going to win. And finally, after a grueling fight, I got there. I arrived at the finish line. I reached the egg victorious and I was conceived!

I know it sounds crazy, but think about it. We were all once just a tiny little sperm that had to defeat thousands, if not millions, of others to be born. We had to fight. We had to persevere. We had to triumph. You don't defeat millions unless you have something special within you. You must have an innate ability to succeed and an indomitable will.

You see we all, from our very beginnings, are winners. We defeated millions because we wanted it more. We were destined to win. We have this ability still within us to this very day. Sometimes people just forget that we have this Power within. We forget that with great focus and dedication we can accomplish fantastic feats.

People sometimes stop believing in themselves and they stop trusting their instincts. They forget that they can do ALL things through the Almighty Power within which strengthens them. You have the Gift. You had It from the very beginning. The Power and the Energy is still in you. Believe in it.

MIND
CLEANSE

Viruses

Just like a computer is prone to viruses, the mind can also be invaded and infected by negative influences which prevent it from doing all it is capable of doing. Unfortunately, most people have already allowed viruses to intrude their mind. These viruses have poisoned most of us and have kept us from being able to operate optimally. These invaders of mind have prevented us from achieving the greatness we are meant to achieve. In their simplest form, the viruses of our Mind are anything negative. Much like the spyware and adware that can infect and disable your laptop, the invaders of your mind must be identified and then removed so that you can operate optimally once again like you were meant to. What are some examples of these viruses, negative influences and invaders of Mind? I believe that there are two different strains of viruses that can creep in and infect our Minds. Each of these strains contains three sub-strains.

EXTERNAL VIRUSES:

Come from our surroundings and creep into our minds through the five senses.

Negative People:

Pessimists, complainers, whiners, gossipers

Negative Places:

Time: After 10:30pm

Place: Bars, restaurants, clubs, parties

Substance: Drugs or alcohol

Negative Propaganda:

Magazines, television, social media, advertisements

INTERNAL VIRUSES:

Cripple us from within through inferior thoughts and belief systems.

Doubt:

- The opposite of Faith
- Negative self-talk infects our minds from within with phrases like: "I can't do it", "I'm not good enough"

Hopelessness:

Pessimism, negative outlook on life's circumstances

Fear:

The opposite of Love, being afraid, the greatest hindrance to the proper execution of all physical action

The greatest of the negative influences is fear. Fear is the greatest hindrance to the achievement of our goals. My mom often reminds me of a quote from Robert Schuller that snaps me back to reality every time I hear it: "What would you attempt to do if you knew you would not fail?"

I strongly encourage you to make a list right now. If not on paper, mentally, take note of all the viruses in your life. What are they? Who are they? What are you afraid of?

Robert Schuller is a retired American televangelist, speaker and motivator. He has written over 37 books, six of which have been named to the "The New York Times" bestseller's list.

Negative influences of the mind prevent us from being the best we can be. They are the thorns of our thought-life, the defects of our decision-making and the glitches in our game-planning. When there is no sense of ease in our mind, it is the negative influences that cause the dis-ease; nasty little hindrances those are.

Imagine that your mind is a bucket. What kind of water (thoughts) have you been putting in your bucket? Have you been putting good, clean, pure and healthy water in your bucket? Would you share the water you've been collecting with those you care about? If not, you have been putting dirty, infectious and contaminated water in your bucket. This type of harmful water can be detrimental to your health and happiness. Not only can this water be damaging to you but it can also harm those around you. Those who come to you and seek your presence can be harmed by what comes out of you.

Instead of a bucket, maybe you could imagine your Mind to be a mirror that has been sitting in a dark closet for years. Without realizing that you were keeping your mirror in the dark, it has accumulated many cobwebs and layers of dust (negativity) that has completely covered the mirror.

The full potential and ability of the mirror has been clouded. Now that you realize that you have not been caring for your mirror, you can take it out of the darkness and wipe it completely clean, removing all of the dust and negativity so that it can once again be a perfect reflection of the Light and all that is GOoD. Your Pure Mind can shine bright once again.

We must learn to remove the dust from our mirror so that we may shine bright. We must remove all of the negative entities that have been preventing us from reaching our full potential. We must no longer carry infectious water around in our brain-bucket.

Mind Cleanse: Rub-A-Dub-Dub, Your brain in a tub.

What Has Been Programming Your Mind?

Look at most reality shows and you will see in a nutshell what society has chosen to highlight, embrace, condone and relish. Turn on the nightly news and you will see an entire show talking about murder, scandal, violence and hate. Turn on your radio and you will hear songs about lying, cheating, drinking, smoking, gambling and wasting money on strippers. Everywhere you look or listen in today's world you will find negativity.

We are inundated with uselessness every day. So, it's no wonder that our Minds have been programmed to think about and focus on negativity. Whatever we see, hear, touch, taste and smell on a daily basis affects us. Our five senses are avenues through which the outside world can gain access to our Minds. We are the Keeper at the gate, and we decide whether or not we will let something we see or hear come in and affect us.

To some degree, all of the influences you've allowed to creep in and affect your Mind have shaped you into the person you are. Your entire life you have been programming your Mind. You have created the person that is reading this book. The person you are right now is the result of the state of Mind you've kept and the decisions you've made.

Whether you realize it or not, you have been creating your future too. Maybe you realize that you create your own world, but what you may not be aware of are all the influences that have been shaping your world unbeknownst to you. You may not realize that there are many hidden influences that have been affecting your state of Mind and manipulating your decisions.

You may not be aware of all the "ball and chains" which you have allowed to enter your Mind, those burdens that subconsciously govern your life. One vital key to knowing thyself is being able to understand all of the influences in your life that shape and affect your state of Mind. The people we communicate with, the songs we listen to, the television shows and movies we watch and the books and magazines we read are all major influencers of our state of Mind.

Each and every day, these influences have been shaping your state of Mind. Are the people you're hanging around positive, uplifting, inspirational and loving people who make you better? Or, as Jon Gordon calls them, are they "energy vampires" filled with negativity that drains you of your happiness? Do the people you spend your time with curse up a

Jon Gordon is an American motivational speaker and author of six books. He coined the term "energy vampires" in his book "The Energy Bus".

storm and complain and whine about everything and everybody? What do the lyrics in the songs you listen to do to your Mind? Do they fill your Mind with positive energy? Do they recite verses and lyrics that will program you to be the type of person you wish to be? What types of movies and TV shows do you watch? What images and words are written in the books and magazines you read?

All of the images, words, and thoughts that enter your Mind affect you. We must learn to be cognizant, in every moment, of that with which we surround ourselves! Guard your gnosis. Barricade your brain.

We conform to that with which we surround ourselves. Think

about a room full of people and one person yawns. How long does it take before multiple people yawn? Not long, right?

If you spend a lot of your time taking garbage into your Mind, it's only a matter of time before you start getting garbage out of your Mind. The opposite is true too, of course.

There was a time in my life when I was hanging out with the wrong crowd. I'm not saying that the people I was hanging out with were bad people, but they were just doing things that I didn't need to be doing. These people were influencing the way I thought, the way I acted and the decisions I made. I wasted a lot of time hanging around people who weren't influencing me in a positive way. Instead of giving me strength, they were making me weaker, both mentally and spiritually.

Humans are so easily influenced by their surroundings that it's scary. Every day, whether we realize it or not, our Minds are being influenced by our surroundings. If your Mind is a computer, imagine that your surroundings install programs into your Mind. These programs govern your thoughts and your thoughts then influence your words and actions. These installed programs have a huge influence over our lives.

Because most of us do not realize this is what has been happening to us all our lives, our poor Minds have taken quite a bit of abuse. Our Minds are so inundated with crap and negativity that if we were to open up our brains and take a peek it would look and smell like a big pile poo. All the negative words, images and thoughts that we've allowed to creep in are crippling us; they are preventing us from becoming the very best that we can be.

Because we have not been aware of the negative thoughts, words and images that have crept into our Minds, our Minds are filled with fear, doubt and worry.

- We fear that we are not capable of being great. We lack confidence because negative people have told us that we are not good enough.

- We doubt ourselves because we do not believe in our own abilities. We have not trained ourselves to have the Mind of a champion.

- We worry because we do not have the peace of Mind that comes from knowing that we have done everything we could have possibly done to set ourselves up for success.

The more deeply embedded a fear, doubt or negative thought is programmed in your mind, the more difficult it is to remove the restraint. Negative thinking and self-doubt have become the norm for most of us. Our own negative thoughts and beliefs are the things that hold us back the most.

Brainwash Yourself

Before we can begin to reprogram our Minds for greatness we must clear it of all clutter, all the rubbish and negativity that is hindering us from being all that we are meant to be. Emptying our Mind reminds me of a Zen proverb that discusses how our Minds are like a teacup.

"Once, a long time ago, there was a wise Zen master. People from far and near would seek his counsel and ask for his wisdom. Many would come and ask him to teach them, enlighten them in the way of Zen. He seldom turned any away.

One day an important man, a man used to command and obedience came to visit the master. "I have come today to ask you to teach me about Zen. Open my mind to enlightenment." The tone of the important man's voice was that of one used to getting his own way. The Zen master knew that he was dealing with a "know it all."

The Zen master smiled and said that they should discuss the matter over a cup of tea. When the tea was served the master poured his visitor a cup. He poured and he poured and the tea rose to the rim and began to spill over the table and finally onto the robes of the wealthy man. Finally the visitor shouted, 'Enough. You are spilling the tea all over. Can't you see the cup is full?'

The master stopped pouring and smiled at his guest. 'You are like this tea cup, so full that nothing more can be added. Come back to me when the cup is empty. Come back to me with an empty mind'"

The term "brainwash" has always had such a negative connotation, but it does not necessarily have to be negative; instead of "brainwashing" let's call it "Mindcleansing". When we Mindcleanse we do three things:

1. We clear our Minds of what we have been told was possible.

2. We get rid of unnecessary Mind clutter & negative thought patterns.

3. We make room for GOoD.

It is essential that we Mindcleanse so that we can then reprogram our mind and fill it with positive thought patterns. This process is one of the greatest secrets to achieving all that you wish to achieve.

I encourage you to empty your teacup. When tea sits too long it develops a sour taste as a result of bacteria growth. When negativity steeps in our mind, over a course of time, infection sets in disabling Divine Design. Empty that cup and fill it with fresh brew. Wipe the Mind clean of past negativity. Reprogram it for success.

If you want to help yourself on your mission, you'll want to keep yourself well-conditioned

This next secret deals with being able to recognize and acknowledge those moments when you allow a negative thought, word or deed to creep into your realm of existence. We must train ourselves to whip those demons when they come around creepin'. We often allow improper thoughts, words and deeds to slide by unregulated. When we do not correct ourselves we are giving ourselves a green light to continue committing those crimes of our minds. What we accept, we condone.

If you think a bad thought, you should correct yourself. If you say a bad word, or do a bad deed, you should reprimand yourself. If you doubt yourself, reroute yourself. If you offend yourself, amend yourself. If you think, say or do anything negative, you should SNAP YOURSELF. If you get caught in a negative pattern of thought, you need to SNAP OUT OF IT.

When I was growing up, my parents would not let me say any curse words. Four-letter words were a big no-no. There was one four-letter word however, that was the worst of them all: "can't".

It makes me feel like my fingers are dirty just typing that word. Why did my parents say this was the worst four-letter word of all of them? All the four-letter curse words are used to curse someone else. The "c-word", "can't", however, puts a curse on yourself. It is literally putting a curse on you, just like a witch putting a hex or curse on you, keeping you from achieving, or doing, that which you actually CAN. If you say you "can't" do something, you have given up. If you say you "can't" be something, then you have no faith in yourself.

My parents made a rule that any time I said that word I would immediately have to do ten push-ups. It didn't matter if we were at home or at the shopping mall, if I said it, I was doing push-ups. As you can imagine, it didn't take long

Behavior modification techniques are designed to alter an individual's behaviors and reactions through positive and negative reinforcement. The reinforcement often involves learning adaptive behavior that includes in some cases a removal of undesired behavior. It's also known as "classical conditioning", a form of learning first demonstrated by 19th-century Russian psychologist Ivan Pavlov. Pavlov used the sound of bells and electric shock to induce anticipatory reactions for food in dogs.

before I realized that it did not behoove me to say that word. I still do ten push-ups to this day, and some of my closest friends do it now too!

At first it was difficult to refrain from cursing myself with that word. Eventually my parents' technique worked. They conditioned me to not only refrain from saying it, but after some time I didn't even think it. After my parents conditioned me to no longer use the "c" word, I was more hopeful, faithful and powerful. Anything was possible, even my wildest dreams. So how were my parents able to condition me to never use that word? The push-ups!!! They trained me by using a behavior modification technique, specifically, punishing me every time I did something they did not want me to do.

How can we apply this training technique to our own lives? Much like good ol' Pavlov and his dogs taught us, through classical conditioning, we can train ourselves to snap out of bad habits. Pavlov zapped his dogs and they learned. When you catch yourself thinking, or acting, sub-optimally you are going to zap yourself too.

Get yourself a Change Your Mind Bracelet on my website, and put it on your wrist. Any time you catch yourself thinking bad thoughts, saying crippling/cursing words or doing a bad deed, SNAP YOURSELF! If you're trying to stop cursing, but a bad word slips out, SNAP YOURSELF! If you're trying to lose weight, but you catch yourself thinking about eating bad foods, SNAP YOURSELF! If you have a goal to achieve, but you find yourself doubting your abilities, SNAP YOURSELF!

When you correct yourself, it acknowledges and brings awareness to the fact that you will not stand for sub-optimal behavior any longer. This is how you condition yourself to be able to conquer those destructive ways and not let moments of weakness pass by unaddressed. Soon you will learn to do away with those destructive ways completely. Those crippling and disabling ways will be stopped before they ever have a chance to gain momentum and influence.

I wouldn't have the discipline that I have today if it weren't for my karate master growing up. Grand Master Young Ui Min, sporting his 9th degree black belt, would drag me all around the dojo by my ear if I did not listen to instruction. I wouldn't tell the truth like I do today if it weren't for the bar of soap that my dad made me eat when I was caught lying. We have all been conditioned one way or another in our lives. We must use this powerful training technique to train our minds to be disciplined and tough.

This type of MindTraining works. We soon learn to control our thoughts and be aware of the disabling thoughts, words and deeds that we allow into our lives. We condition ourselves to act with purpose and correctness. When we catch ourselves thinking negatively we SNAP OUT OF IT! Every thought, even the smallest one, matters.

Every idle word that men shall speak, they shall give account thereof in the Day of Judgment.

— Matthew12.36

Born Again

I'm here to tell you that no matter how bad you've been to yourself, no matter how much rubbish you've allowed to creep into your Mind or how bad the naysayers have been to you, you can get rid of all the negativity that has crept in and polluted your Mind. You can wipe it all away. You can Mindcleanse yourself so that you can start fresh and new!

When someone asks when our birthday is, our reply should always be, "Tomorrow morning!" It may sound a little crazy, but we can then proceed to tell them that each day we are born again. The dawn of each new day brings the ability to wipe the slate clean of all the wrongs we have done to ourselves and others. Each day we have the ability to repent from all the bad thoughts we have had and negative actions we have committed. If we are to ever be completely happy, we must free ourselves of our pasts.

Very truly I tell you, no one can see the kingdom of God unless they are born again

-John 3:3

Christians believe that people need to be cleansed from their sins to experience Heaven. In the Bible it says to repent. They are encouraged to be sorry for, and to turn away from, their sinful habits.

What does it mean to repent? When we repent, we have a complete change of heart because of a feeling of remorse for the wrong we've done in our past; wrong to others, yes, but especially the wrong we have done to ourSelves.

The very definition of "repentance" explains it clearly. When you seek repentance you are changing your mind. It is a change that involves turning away from all the wrong we have done (to ourselves and others) and vowing to dedicate ourSelves to the amendment of our life. When we make the commitment to turn from our evil ways, we get a feeling of freedom. We get a strong sense of being in control of our lives.

Once you forgive yourself and realize that all the bad you have done in your past is over and done with you will no longer feel condemned by the wrongs you've done. You feel quite empowered. You will experience a sense of joy which stems from the realization that you can choose to no longer partake of negative ways. A huge weight is lifted off the shoulders of your collective conscience.

You will realize that at that point you can move on. Once you free yourself from your past and forgive yourself for all that you have done, you will be able to start fresh and new. When you allow yourself to be reborn, it is as if the slate has been wiped completely clean and you can start a new life and a new way of living from there on out. When you relieve your own conscience of the massive buildup of guilt, you will be vindicated.

When collective guilt bogs you down, mental strain and torment is your crown. You must free yourself from your own mind. Realize that you are no longer going to be imprisoned by your own past negative thoughts and perceptions of yourself.

Let's be honest here. When we screw up, it really bugs us. We may try to play it off, justify it, blame it on someone else and say that they deserved it, but no matter how hard we try, it eats away at us. Realize that you can free yourSelf from those bonds. Simply put, you can replace the negativity with positivity.

Not only do we poison our own minds, but often others are the perpetrators. We have all had people whose purpose in life was to, seemingly, bring us down. According to all the haters when I was growing up there was no way I should have ever made it to the NFL. If I had a dollar for every time someone said that I couldn't do it I'd be Bill Gates rich. When I was in high school all I heard was, "Well, he's pretty good but he's not fast enough for college." Then, when I got a full scholarship to Stanford University and started playing Division I football all I heard was, "Well, he's pretty good as a college player, but he definitely won't make it to the NFL." Then, when I got drafted by the Buffalo Bills in the third round of the draft I heard them say, "Well, he somehow got drafted, but it was a fluke and he doesn't have what it takes. He'll never last."

Here I am, after having played nine years in the NFL, mostly as team captain for the teams for which I've played. Not bad for a little, part-Asian kid from central Pennsylvania who was never big enough, fast enough, strong enough or the right skin color to be a good football player!

I once had a group of people, who I thought were my friends, ostracize me. As their envy grew, so did their desire to put me down and spread false rumors about me. They spread rumors that I was using drugs like cocaine and crack. They were spreading rumors that I was using steroids. I once gave one of my best friends $15,000 in thanks for helping me prepare for my rookie year in the NFL. That same friend then asked me for a Corvette and, later, more money. After refusing, that same "friend" tried to sabotage me and ruin my reputation.

The point to all of this is that we will always have negative influences in our life. Whether they are negative people or influences such as alcohol, drugs, TV or video games, there will always be unfavorable forces in our life. There's no stopping their existence. Those opposing pressures will never go away but we can cleanse ourselves of all the negativity that has poisoned us up until this point in our lives. Once we've Mindcleansed ourselves, all we have to do is remain conscious of all the negative influences in our lives and guard ourselves from them so they will not affect us moving forward.

Most people in our society carry around an agitated state of mind almost every day of their lives. I once heard that our true pure and peaceful Mind is like a pearl at the bottom of the ocean. Most people cannot look down at the water and see the pearl clearly because the surface of the water has many waves. These waves and ripples in the water are whipped by the winds of agitation. We must learn to calm the waves so that the mind is serene and anyone can see the pearl clearly.

Imagine your Mind as a chalkboard that has years' worth of

rubbish and graffiti all over it. By realizing that all of the rubbish is there, and that it is useless and obstructive, you can take your eraser and wipe the slate clean. You can clear away all the crap so that there is a clean slate, a clear Mind with which you can now work.

We've only been given one precious Mind. If we want to be the best that we can be we must utilize all of it. We need every part of our Mind to be filled with positive energy and uplifting thoughts if we are going to be able to do all that we are capable of doing. We must rid our minds of the viruses that we have allowed to creep in and cripple us from within; the viruses that have fooled us into thinking that we are inferior, insufficient and incapable. The world in which we live is difficult enough as it is without us getting in our own way.

We are surrounded daily by many external challenges. If our aim is to be the best we can be then we should not allow anything negative to clutter our minds and hinder us internally. Mind clutter will only make life's difficulties seem worse than they already are. Any negative influences we allow to intrude our minds will become additional obstacles that make reaching our goals even more difficult. We will never reach our maximum potential, accomplish all that we were meant to accomplish and attain the glory and success that is rightfully ours if we don't rid ourselves of the mental hindrances that keep us from reaching our full potential. Just as computers get viruses, our mind can also be invaded and infected by negative influences. Don't let that pressure get to you. Don't let that bad habit hold you back. Don't let that wretched person influenced by all the garbage coming in bother you! You have to practice Mindcleansing.

Do not conform to the pattern of this world, but be transformed by the renewing of your mind.

— ROMANS 12:2

RETRAIN
YOUR BRAIN

Reap What You Sow

Now that you have realized that the trash in your Mind has been crippling you and you've learned to rid yourself of it all, you will have a clearer Mind to work your life's Magic. No longer do you have to wander aimlessly through life. No longer do you have to mope through the years on autopilot. No longer must you be imprisoned, doing time in your own Mind, suffering from your own arrested development. No longer must you be governed by outside influences that are shaping you into someone you have not consciously chosen to be.

Now because you have a clearer Mind, you are at the point where you can consciously choose the programs that you will put into your Mind. You can consciously choose to have positive, uplifting and motivational programs running in your Mind that will empower you and propel you towards success at an alarming rate.

Are you ready to fulfill your purpose? Are you ready to reach your maximum potential? All you have to do is reprogram your Mind!

Since you were young people have been telling you what you

can and, mostly, what you cannot do. Now however, you realize that it doesn't matter what others have said. You also know now that it doesn't matter that you have wasted hundreds of hours watching pointless TV shows, poking people on Facebook and playing computer or video games. You are in control of your Mind now.

There's no more autopilot for you. You are the Pilot of your Mind and it's time to steer this vessel to the exact destination that you want. You are going to set your sights on the goals you have set for yourself and you are going to go soaring towards success.

You are now back to your original nature. You are capable of all things. You can and will achieve anything you're strong enough in your mind to achieve.

The Mind is everything. What you think, you become.

-Siddharta Gautama

Why is it important to reprogram our minds? In the heat of the moment, when the game is on the line, when you are in the interview for the job of your dreams or when you meet that special person you've been waiting for, your thoughts and actions will be influenced by the programs you have installed into your subconscious Mind.

We must be careful what we program into our Minds. Whatever we tell our subconscious Mind we are, or whatever we tell it we can do, it will take for fact and work it out accordingly. If a man has a garden and he plants cucumber seeds, cucumbers will grow. If that same man sows grape seeds, he will eventually reap grape vines.

If you tell yourself you will fail or don't allow yourself to believe you can succeed, the odds will be against you before you even begin. The same is true if you hear about your pending failure from others and believe it, you will never succeed.

Olympic hurdlers must believe they will clear every hurdle in every race in order to do so; otherwise they leave the clearance of the hurdles to chance. If a golfer can think only of avoiding hitting the ball into the water, it's likely that a shot into the water is in his future. Smokers who repeatedly say they can't quit aren't setting themselves up for the success of quitting smoking. You will do and become anything you believe, whether it impacts your life positively or negatively.

> ## If we say it long enough eventually we're going to reap a harvest. We're going to get exactly what we're saying.
>
> -Joel Osteen

Our subconscious Mind is the Captain of the ship (in this case the ship is our body). That Captain takes orders very well and performs those orders with precision and accuracy. Whatever we tell our subconscious Mind repeatedly with our thoughts, or the things we watch or listen to, the subconscious Mind will absorb. It will then give those exact orders to the body which always obeys. When a thought pattern or idea is deeply engrained in the subconscious Mind, the body can carry out the orders it was given without even thinking about what to do.

> Your conscious mind may slumber. It may be rendered impotent by anesthetics or a sudden blow. But your subconscious mind works on.
>
> -Robert Collier

During my second year in the NFL with the Buffalo Bills, in a game against the Detroit Lions, I had to face their big running back, James Stewart, head-to-head. It was third-and-1, the quarterback gave Stewart the ball and he started barreling towards the line of scrimmage. I lowered my head and blasted him with everything I had. The collision gave Stewart a shattered shoulder and he never played football again.

I had a concussion, but kept playing, essentially unconscious and unaware of what I was doing. Although I had no recollection of what followed, I played four more plays after that collision.

I sacked the quarterback, dropped back into pass coverage a couple of times and almost blocked the fourth-down punt. I did all of this essentially unconsciously and I remembered none of it. The next thing I do remember was sitting on the sideline and my teammate Sammy Morris said, "That was an awesome sack!" I replied, "We got a sack?!? That's great! Who got it?" Sammy looked at me with shifty eyes and then immediately yelled for the trainers.

The captain, my subconscious mind, was running the show. My prior physical training sessions in the weight room and on the practice field, combined with my mental training sessions in the film room and classroom allowed me to act decisively and correctly without having to stop, analyze and choose. Because I had trained my brain during practices and film study, I was able to play and perform functions even though I was unconscious. The programs I had installed while I was conscious had taken over when I was unconscious.

It was astonishing and almost unbelievable when I watched the game film the next day. I saw the plays that I had executed while I was unconscious and could not understand how I was able to move and operate at such a high level even though I wasn't consciously choosing to do the tasks. This was yet another experience I had in life that made me realize the power of our Mind. Whatever we program into our minds will manifest.

This is one of the most vital pieces of information I can share with you. If you realize that everything you program into your Mind is shaping and molding you, you can understand how significant each and every one of your thoughts really is. If you program and repeatedly train yourself to be successful, you will be. If you program and train yourself to be average, you will be. How well have you been training your brain?

He who sows sparingly will also reap sparingly, and he who sows bountifully will also reap bountifully

-II Corinthians 9:6

Another example from my life of reaping what you sow happened when I was doing one of my MindCoaching lectures to a few hundred people. Occasionally, I do a routine where I bring up two people and have them do a mental challenge or a game which shows how easily our minds are programmed. I asked for two volunteers and eventually a girl named Tammy and a guy named Derek were standing before me on stage. I told them that they were going to be in a competition and that the winner was going to receive a $20 bill as a prize (I usually only use a $5 bill but this particular time I had forgotten to stop at the bank and lucky for them $20 was all I had!).

Before I ever mentioned anything about mind programming, something incredible happened. I pulled out the $20 from my pocket and as I placed it on the table in front of the two contestants, Tammy, with a look of determination in her eye, muttered under her breath, "I'm gonna win that $20".

I paused immediately and asked her to repeat what she said so that everyone in the audience could hear her. She coyly spoke into the microphone blushing, "I'm going to win that $20". I told the crowd to mark those words. I knew exactly what was about to happen. Sure enough, because of the self-fulfilling prophecy and how she had programmed her mind, Tammy dominated her competition just as I knew she would. Tammy won and Derek never stood a chance.

Are you preventing blessings from occurring in your life? Are you selling yourself short by failing to program your Mind for greatness?

Never, ever sell yourSelf short. With proper programming, your subconscious Mind is capable of doing anything. With proper (re)programming you can do anything that is for GOoD purpose. You can do anything that you program your mind to do.

The Remaining Secret Keys: Author's Note

I have reminded you that you must constantly and consistently rid yourself of past hindrances. You must continually till the soil of your subconscious Mind, getting rid of all the clutter and negative hindrances. It's a never-ending process because this world will always have distractions working to create tangents in your Mind. The Invader of Mind will always be there.

However, now that your conscience is clearer and you have begun to eliminate the negative mental hindrances, you can start to reprogram your Mind with fresh, new, concise, pointed and focused declarations that pertain only to those things you wish to bring into your life. This is the part of the book where I share the remaining Secret Keys that will help you become the person you wish to be. The exciting part of all this is that when you apply these techniques to your life you will see and feel amazing results within weeks.

The next step in the MindTraining process for creating a better You involves using the Secret Keys to reprogram yourself for greatness. You will learn how to plant seeds in the freshly tilled soil of your Mind to produce wonderful and harvestable crops. Some of the methods within this book are the same secrets that the greatest kings, conquerors and masters throughout history have used to achieve greatness. Others are methods that I developed on my own.

I have to warn you; some of these tactics to train your brain are unorthodox. People may say that you're crazy when they see you implementing these methods. People sometimes tell me I'm crazy but I tell them that I'm on a mission. Some of the techniques will be tedious. Remember, in order to be better than most, you have to be willing to do all the little things that most people simply aren't. Appearing crazy is something that most people aren't too comfortable with.

I am excited to share with you some of the tactics I have learned about how to reprogram yourself to have the Mind of magi, the brain of a Brahmin, and the psyche of a sage.

We reap what we sow, so let us sow with purpose, shall we?

To get to where you need to be, see your goals repeatedly.

It's time to start carefully programming your very own Mind. This Secret Key was one of the first that I discovered and utilized to get what I wanted in life. I was taught this Secret Key at a very young age by my Mother.

When I was as young as 14 years old, I can remember waking up every morning as almost every teenager does with dread by the thought of having to go to school. It was so early and all I wanted to do was sleep. After begrudgingly forcing myself out of bed, I would take the ten routine steps to the bathroom to brush my teeth. But as soon as I would get to the bathroom my mood would change. There, on the mirror in the bathroom, would be a Post-it note with an inspirational quote written on it.

My Mom, Jane, had placed an inspirational quote that would

change my entire mood. What could have been a boring, tiresome and negative day was instantly transformed into an exciting, lively and positive day with tremendous possibilities from the very beginning. A shift in Consciousness and attitude occurred because of the positive thoughts and inspirational words that my Mom left for me. Positive programs were installed in my mind at the beginning of each new day.

The quotes my Mother left on my bathroom mirror were about gratitude, some about faith and others about perseverance, but all of them were positive and uplifting. Some were written by famous authors or poets and some were written by my Mother. Each of them would remain on the mirror for about a week. Then, after some time there would be another. I still have a recipe holder that contains all the quotes. I now realize the genius in what my Mom was doing. She was programming my Mind with positivity. The more I saw positive words and phrases, the better I felt! I took this philosophy and ran with it.

I started to write messages of positivity everywhere. I would write them all over my body, especially my hands and wrists. When the weather got warm and I could wear shorts, I would write them on my thigh below my shorts line so that when I was sitting in class I would see it and be reminded of my goals and my mission. Every time I would catch a glimpse of the magic words they would influence my decisions in that moment. They would influence what I said and what I did or did not do depending on the situation.

My inspirational words were mood-changers too. If I was sad, or even tired, those words often changed my Mind. No matter where I went or what I did, I had a constant reminder of the person I was trying to be. When you have that constant reminder of a goal or desired state of Mind in front of you, that impetus keeps you focused on what decisions you should make and what things you should say or not say. They hold us accountable to be the person we want to be. Those words will be our constant reminders to help keep us on track.

Even today I have inspirational messages written on my skin. The "tattoos" are powerful messages to me personally and they resonate within my Soul. What I believe within, I embed in my skin. These truths are personal motivation techniques that serve as a constant reminder of the person I aim to be.

My first year in the NFL, I even went so far as to put reminders on the hats and clothing that I wore. I remember going to the mall to buy a hat and I would see all these teams and brands and logos that meant nothing to me. Why would I wear something that said nothing about who I am? Why would I wear a hat that would project to myself and others, an image that did not represent who I am and where I am going? When you wear clothing you are portraying a message about who you are to others. Your clothing is a representation of the type of person that you are. Whether you realize it or not, the way you dress and the things you adorn yourself with say a lot about you. In a world where first impressions are very important, it is crucial to carefully choose how we portray ourselves. We must discerningly determine the vibe we give off to others.

Knowing this, I had to do something about my desire to wear a hat, but not be conflictingly branded. Here's what I did:

I decided that I wanted to have a customized hat made. I wanted a hat that had my own words on it. I wanted to have my own positive messages embroidered on it so that when I wore it people would have a better understanding of who I am and what I am about. Most importantly, it would be a constant reminder to myself of who I am.

So I had the Chinese symbol for progress, Chien, embroidered on a hat. Every time I caught a glimpse of that symbol, while wearing the hat in the weight room, it would instantly break up the monotony of the workout. As you know, it's easy to just go through the motions once you start exercising. Instead of working out without the necessary intensity, I would instantly be rejuvenated and refreshed with the thought that I was going to make progress. I had places to go and I had goals I wanted to achieve. My actions in the weight room were all part of the process of progress to get me there.

I eventually started to put these messages, words, and reminders on my shirts, too. A few of my favorite T-shirts that I wear are: "Believe", "On a Mission", "Blessed", "SOULdier" and "HIStory in the Making". You can find some of these MindTraining shirts on my website, www.coywire.com.

These shirts are reminders of who I am. Not only does wearing the shirts serve as a reminder for me when I catch a glimpse of the words, they also prove to be wonderful conversation starters with other people who notice the words. To this very day, I meet some of the most positive people one would ever want to meet because they see the shirt, smile and then ask where I got it. A single word or phrase has the power behind it to change not only your mindset, but others' as well. Put your vibe out into the universe. It's your frequency and let others tune in.

I needed, and still need, these positive re-enforcers in my life because my own mind is my own worst enemy.

We have to re-mind our minds, discipline them and keep them in line. We need constant reminders that keep us motivated, positive, and moving toward the direction of our goals. Every time we catch a glimpse of them in public situations, where negative influences may surround us, they remind us to stay focused, positive, and disciplined. They remind us that it would not behoove us to do everything that others may choose to do. They are not going where we are trying to go, and therefore we cannot do all that they choose to do. Put words EVERYWHERE. This technique is one of the best you can use to help you change your Mind.

Your Repetition Mission:

The number of times you've said it, will determine where you're headed.

Purpose: To keep your mission on your mind at all times. It's easy to go through a day and be distracted by inferior influences and people and forget to live righteously for those ideals you hold in your mind as mental pictures. When you catch glimpses of your notes, words and mantras, you are reminded of all that you are and all that you are trying to be. Once we know what it is we are setting out to accomplish in our lives, we must surround ourselves with reminders so that we don't stray too far from our goals. Especially in our moments of weakness, these self- motivation techniques will keep us inspired and on track.

A few ways to remind yourself of who you are and what you want to be are:

- Post-its with motivational phrases everywhere your eyes will look
- Written words of inspiration and motivation on your hands, thighs and forearms
- Shirts with words of inspiration and positivity
- Written motivational words and quotes on a card carried in your pocket, wallet or purse.

Choices, Decisions & Consequences

A man is what he thinks about all day long.

— Ralph Waldo Emerson

Choices, decisions and consequences are the way all things work in this world. We have choices every day that require decisions on how we will respond and act, and from those decisions come the consequences.

What you will be one year, three years and five years from now depends on what you think today. If you learn to accept this and make it work for you in your life, you become the puppet master of your own life, pulling the string for anything you desire.

Life presents CHOICES.

We make DECISIONS.
Decisions determine our DESTINY.

We are decision-makers in every second of our lives. Decisions we make in this moment determine the outcome of our hours. Those hours become days and weeks, which become the years that make up our life. The decisions we make in this moment will shape the outcome of our entire lives. Are you really that powerful? Yes you are, so you must decide wisely.

The butterfly effect is the theory that even the smallest actions set into motion a series of events that cause great outcomes. Even the slight movement of air caused by the flap of a butterfly's wings in Pennsylvania can set into motion a series of movements and reactions that end up causing a hurricane halfway around the world in India. That is the same law that governs our Mind. Our smallest thoughts, even the seemingly insignificant thoughts, set into motion a series of reactions that shape our future. You are more powerful than you know. You have the ability to choose and become anything you want. When you take control of your thoughts, you take control of your entire life.

Mike Dooley is a former international tax consultant turned author of books on spiritual accountability published in 25 languages. Dooley now travels the world speaking about achieving your life's wildest dreams and finding happiness in everything.

As Mike Dooley says, "thoughts become things." This is a law of the universe. It is an unchangeable law that governs all of our lives whether we choose to realize it or not. Our thoughts shape the reality we experience every day. Our thoughts create the person you see in the mirror. Dooley said, "Thoughts become things all the time, not some of the time." All thoughts, the positive and negative ones, become things. That is why we must constantly monitor the thoughts we allow in our Minds. We must constantly cultivate positive thoughts within our Minds and immediately cast out any negative thought that tries to enter our Mind. Focus on positive thoughts, words, actions and feelings that are working to create the successful life you desire.

Watch your thoughts, for
they become words.
Watch your words, for they become actions.
Watch your actions, for they become habits.
Watch your habits, for they
become character.
Watch your character, for it becomes
your destiny.

-Author Unknown

Create a Mantra

Program the destination with empowered declarations

You must create a mantra for your life. Consider it a mission statement for the business of your life.

A mantra is a phrase that is capable of creating transformation. Tibetan Buddhist monks recite a certain mantra because, spiritually, they have a destination they want to get to. They want to reach enlightenment, their version of Heaven. Their mantra is: "Om mani padme hum. Om mani padme hum. Om mani padme hum." Over and over they repeat that mantra for many hours to help them reach the destination. Catholics recite Hail Marys and The Lord's Prayer repeatedly for penance and religious focus. They believe that repeating these powerful mantras will bring them closer to God.

We too must create a mantra for our lives. However, our phrase is not going to be one that has to take us all the way to

God. Our mantra will be a phrase that helps bring us closer to our goals. If mantras are used by others to draw nearer to God, isn't it likely that a mantra will more easily draw us closer to the proximity of our goals?

Your mantra will be a thoughtfully formulated phrase that is designed to keep you honed in on your goals. You will repeat it over and over to constantly reMind yourself where you want to go, who you are becoming and who you want to be. You must formulate a phrase that will evoke the Spirit of the person you wish to become. Remember, your thoughts create your reality; therefore, you must take control of and direct your thoughts.

Your personal mantra is a great way to affirm to yourself, repeatedly, a desired goal or purpose for your life. When you have goals that you want to achieve, it is critically important to reMind yourself every day of those goals so that they are in the forefront of your Mind. You must make your goals your priority if you are ever going to give them the attention and energy they need to come to fruition.

Mantras are used to implant, embed, engrain and sow desired thought patterns in your Mind. Mantras help you change your Mind. The more often you say, hear or see your goals and the more time you invest in contemplating them, the more important they will become to you.

Like one of my former defensive coordinators, Brian Van-Gorder, once said, "The more time you invest into something, the more important it becomes to you."

When your goals become more important to you, you will start

COY WIRE • WWW.COYWIRE.COM

reprioritizing your life. You will start making all the necessary updates that are required for change. You may begin to realize those TV shows aren't quite as important as they used to be. You may realize that the people you were spending a lot of time with were a big waste of your most precious commodity: your time. You might realize that you could be eating better and sleeping more.

My mantra when I was in college was: "The Spirit of the Lord lives and moves in all that I say and do. I am a leader, a Souldier and the best athlete in the NFL draft."

This was a powerful phrase that I carried with me wherever I went. It contained all of my deepest desires at that particular point in my life. After much contemplation, those were the words that I chose to direct my life. Your mantra could include a spiritual aspect, a family/community aspect and a specific career aspect. It should be simple, it should flow, it should feel good and it should sound good when you say it. You are programming yourself to be the person you want to be so go for it! Create your mantra, get it right, get it precise and get it perfect. Be sure that you say the things as if you already are that which you wish to be. For example, if you want to be successful, say, "I am successful" as opposed to "I want to be successful." If in your mantra you say that you WANT to be successful, you will get exactly that. You will always be WANTing; you will never actually be. Pick the exact words in your mantra that will help shape your destiny.

We must repeat our mantra over and over, all day long. If creating our mantra was sowing, or planting, the desired goal into our Minds, then repeating it over and over is like watering that seed so that it will grow rapidly. The more we say and hear our mantra, the more it becomes us. Every waking hour, we should aim to say our mantra in our Mind several times. When we are able, we should also say the mantra aloud. Even when we are in public places and there are people around us we should be focused on our purpose. Repeating our mantra helps us to hold our purpose firmly in our Mind. When distractions come we will be less likely to acknowledge them or be affected by them if we have our mantra fresh on our Minds. It will become the kryptonite to any hindrances that could possibly keep us from our goals. When we are alone, it is recommended that we say our mantra out loud and repeat it over and over.

Napoleon Hill is a 20th-century American author and considered one of the earliest writers of self-help books on the topic of personal success. His book "Think and Grow Rich" is one of the best-selling books of all time with over 20 million copies sold. He was an advisor to President Franklin D. Roosevelt from 1933-1936.

Many have tried this technique and failed to achieve their goals. They realized that the point of this technique was to implant upon your subconscious Mind the thought of what it is you desire, but simply seeing and saying your goals over and over is not enough. There is one key ingredient to this secret that you can't overlook. You can say your goal until you are blue in the face, but you will not get the results you want unless you incorporate this vital detail that Napoleon Hill stated best:

Your subconscious mind recognizes

and acts only upon thoughts which have been well-mixed with emotion and feeling.

Thank goodness I have darkly tinted windows, because it reduces the chances of people noticing me chant my mantra, not that I really care anyway. There are probably thousands of people out there, who at some point passed me on the highway, not knowing who I was, and went home to their family and said, "You should've seen this guy driving his car on the highway today, I think he was delusional."

You see, I've found that the best time for me to chant my mantra is while driving in the car. I'm all alone and I won't disturb the neighbors or scare the cats. I need to be alone because when I chant my mantra I really get into it. I feel like I am The Wizard of Oz, standing behind the curtain, and in my most passionate, thundering and intimidating voice, I belt my mantra and force it upon my subconscious Mind with conviction, power and passion. I feel as if I am the lead role back in the days when Shakespeare was still alive, and I pour all of my heart and soul into each and every line. I am like a fiery-eyed flamenco dancer stomping my purpose and goals into the depths of my Mind with every recitation. I even get goose bumps.

I've found that one of the body's natural reactions to pure passion is the phenomenon of goose bumps. Whether you feel it yourself or witness it in another who is experiencing it, you know you're in the presence of passion when a surge comes over your body so Power-full that it causes goose bumps. You must get your emotion involved.

Model yourself after your favorite actor. Have you ever noticed how great actors are able to invoke the spirit of the person they are portraying? That is what you must do. You must get emotionally involved with yourself! You must invoke the Spirit of the person you are striving to be. You must live the part! Win a Grammy for the greatest portrayal of you the world has ever seen.

The good news, and the thing most people don't realize, is that that Spirit, that ability and Power, is already within You. All You have to do is summon It, awaken this sleeping Giant from Its slumber. You must eat, sleep and breathe the person you desire to be. It must consume you. You must ignite yourself and become a man on fire or a woman on fire. You must stoke the flames of the fire that burns inside of you, the fire that has been kindling within ever since you were placed on this Earth.

You see, when you are born unto this Earth within your heart was your good works. You already have within what it takes to accomplish what it is you were sent to accomplish. All you have to do is stoke the flames of your desire until they engulf you. Woven into the very fabric of your entire being must be a belief so strong that you fool yourSelf, and you convince yourSelf that you are that which you desire to be. That is when your belief becomes a reality. That is when you become the person worthy of receiving the title, legitimized as one who deserves the prize, and justified as being qualified enough to receive what you desire.

With our mantra, we are programming our Mind. We are programming our body. We are sending subliminal messages to our Mind all day long. Set an alarm to go off every hour to remind you

COY WIRE • WWW.COYWIRE.COM

to say your mantra in the beginning. Before long you won't need it and that's when you know the programming is working. What we continually sow, we will reap, so start sowing.

Programming is Real

MindProgramming is real and these secret methods actually work. Some of these MindTraining secrets have been hidden from the masses for thousands of years. Why have they been hidden? They are kept hidden for two reasons. The first is that the good people who know the secrets realize that not everyone can be trusted with them. Evil people could use our secret methods for evil purposes. The second reason is that the selfish people who know the secrets want to keep them hidden. The greedy elite don't want others to know about these methods because they want to remain at the top of the food chain and continue to be superior to others.

When you learn how to properly program your Mind, you will open the doorway within that allows the Great Force to enter.

Behold, I stand at the door and knock. If anyone hears My voice and opens the door, I will come in to him and dine with him, and he with Me.

-Revelation 3:20

This Power is amazing. This Great Force that governs all existence flows in and through all of creation. Every man and woman possesses this Power. It is revealed in all the religions of the world. Few great individuals have realized and utilized Its power fully. Those who have were kept under close surveillance. If they began to speak of this Truth and Unlimited Pure Potential, they were cast out and in some cases murdered for the knowledge they possessed and tried to pass on to others. A significant account of this very behavior comes from a well-known Man from Nazareth. This Man had full access to the Power and he wanted to teach the people about it so that they too could have It. The government, the emperor, however, did not want the people to have the Power. They didn't want the people to have the Power because then they wouldn't be able to control them. So, they murdered the Man who was out speaking of the Power.

Walter Payton, Bruce Lee, Martin Luther King Jr. and others began to preach about the Power we possess. Sadly, they are no longer with us either. Can you think of any others throughout history who have tried to preach to others about how Powerful we are? Can you think of anyone who tried to give Power to the masses but they were murdered or mysteriously died at a young age? There have been many who have wanted to share what they had discovered with the masses, but were stopped because there are certain corrupt and wealthy people in positions of power who do not want everyone to know about the TRUTH. They do not want everyone to know about the mighty Power that each of us possesses. If the people had the Power, the wealthy elite would lose their control. In Proverbs 12:23 it says that a prudent man conceals his knowledge. Lao Tsu said that those who know do not say.

Lao Tsu was a philosopher of ancient China and writer of The Tao Te Ching, considered the founding document of Taoism, a belief system based on living in harmony with the Tao, the source of everything that exists.

I believe that it is our birthright to know who we are and of what we are truly capable.

Our world is full of examples of ordinary human beings who have been able to accomplish extra-ordinary feats. Monks who are able to change the temperature of their bodies and slow their heart rate, Shaman who are able to walk on hot coals with bare feet, martial arts masters who can lie on a bed of nails or broken glass without puncturing their skin.

The reason select people are able to do these amazing feats is because they have convinced themselves they are able to do them. They have programmed themselves into believing that they can perform these tasks even though most people would say that it's impossible. Maybe they were never told that these things were impossible or maybe they could care less what others think is possible. Those who are able to achieve extraordinary feats believe they can do the things they set out to do.

People have been programming the mind for years. The big corporations know the power of the mind. They know that the untrained mind, the unguarded mind, is easily programmed. Why do you think they spend millions of dollars on advertising? Why do they use psychological research to choose which colors to use in

COY WIRE • WWW.COYWIRE.COM

their logos? The big corporations and even our own government take advantage of the many who haven't yet been enlightened to the knowledge that all the great civilizations discovered and held sacred. The practice of subliminal advertising was banned in the United Kingdom and Australia. It was also banned by the American networks and the National Association of Broadcasters in 1958. The big corporations, however, still use the knowledge to hypnotize us with their seductive words and images.

Subliminal messages are used to talk to the subconscious Mind while the conscious Mind is completely unaware of it. In the 50's, a man named James Vicary conducted an experiment at a movie theater in Fort Lee, New Jersey. During a movie, Vicary flashed messages such as "Drink Coca-Cola" and "Hungry? Eat Popcorn" on the movie screen every five seconds. The subliminal messages only flashed for 1/3000th of a second at a time. The flash was so obscure and quick that the conscious Mind didn't pick it up. People didn't even realize that they were seeing an image of a Coca-Cola bottle and a suggestive message. The subconscious mind however, picks up everything, recognizes it and records it. Implanted into the subconscious Mind was the mantra "Coke, Coke, Coke...Thirsty, Thirsty, Thirsty! Hungry, Hungry, Hungry... Popcorn Yummy!"

As a result of the subliminal messaging, it was reported that Coca-Cola sales at the theater increased by 18.1% and popcorn purchases increased a whopping 57.8%. This experiment drew a lot of attention. Laws were passed banning subliminal messages. It was thought to be deceptive and a potentially dangerous mind control weapon, even though Vicary later announced that he had fabricated the results of his experiment. I wonder who paid him to say that.

You can look around at advertisements in newspapers, commercials, and magazines and recognize the hidden messages if you are looking for them. Even though some people say that subliminal messaging doesn't work, and even though it's illegal, many advertisers still do it. Big corporations know that sex sells. We've all heard it and we all know that it works. Consider some of the ads you've seen lately and their mental seduction.

The thing we have to realize is that these advertisements aren't accidents. Companies pay hundreds of thousands of dollars on ad campaigns. Every second of a TV commercial has a purpose. Every centimeter of space in a print ad has been carefully plotted and planned.

People who are under hypnosis are able to read text that is backwards, inverted and reversed as if it were written normally. It means that the subconscious Mind decodes any text, no matter how it is written. This meme started circulating over the Internet around 2003. Most people can read this jumbled compilation of letters as long as they keep their eyes progressing steadily through the words:

Olny srmat poelpe can raed this. I cdnuolt blveiee taht I cluod aulaclty uesdnatnrd waht I was rdanieg. The phaonmneal pweor of the hmuan mnid, aoccdrnig to a rscheearch at a mjaor Ui-nervtisy, it deosn't mttaer in waht oredr the ltteers in a wrod are, t he olny iprmoatnt tihng is taht the frist and lsat ltteer be in the rghit pclae. The rset can be a taotl mses and you can sitll raed it wouthit a porbelm. Tihs is bcuseae the huamn mnid deos not raed ervey lteter by istlef, but the wrod as a wlohe. Amzanig huh? yaeh and I awlyas tghuhot slpeling was ipmorantt!

134

Another type of subliminal messaging can be seen in the following illustration. Take a close look to see if you notice anything hidden in the image:

When most people look at an ad, they focus on the image and shapes that are created by the ink, colors and lines. But what must exist for those images and shapes to exist? The answer: blank space. We have been trained to only see the foreground. We often fail to see what is created by the blank space or canvas that

allows the image to exist. Black letters on this paper, for example are able to be seen because of the emptiness behind them. It is the same with sound. In order for sounds to exist, there must be silence. Silence is the blank canvas that allows sound to exist. Although we may not consciously see or hear the background spaces and the emptiness, our subconscious mind sees everything. Some subliminal messages and ads target that part of our brain. You probably did not notice the emptiness, but you should look at the previous image again.

Do you see the word "sex" formed by the white, blank spaces between the flowers? We must not just focus on the images but the blank spaces and empty canvas behind the image that allows the image to exist. It's the same with sounds. Silence is always present. In the emptiness and silence is actually where the Peace is. The same goes for the FedEx logo. Next time you see it, look between the letters for a hidden shape.

Some department stores and supermarkets have actually played subliminal messages under music to reduce shoplifting? In 1979, Time magazine wrote an article entitled, "Secret Voices". The article reported that nearly 50 department stores in the U.S. and Canada had been using subliminal messages over their music systems to reduce shoplifting and employee theft. One East Coast chain was reported to have reduced theft by 37%, amounting to savings of $600,000 over a nine-month period.

Another story in The Wall Street Journal in 1980 stated that subliminal messaging in a New Orleans supermarket resulted in an all-time shoplifting low within the first six months of use. Losses dropped drastically from $50,000 to a figure less than $13,000!

Also, cashier shortages dropped from $125 per week to less than $10 per week. Some examples of the subliminal messages that were used are, "I take a great deal of pride in being honest. I will not steal. I am honest."

A study conducted by the United Nations concluded that "the cultural implications of subliminal indoctrination is a major threat to human rights throughout the world." Why? Because subliminal programming works! If the powers of subliminal messaging were known by all, and the wrong people got ahold of that knowledge they could do bad things, very bad things.

Subliminal programming works. It influences you. It affects your thought patterns, behavior and decision making. Most of us are unconsciously allowing our Minds to be programmed with negativity and smut every day with television programs and advertisements. If you subliminally program negativity into your Mind, you will attract, notice and respond to negativity in your life. If, however, you can learn to program your Mind with good and positivity, then you will be able to transform the world of negativity you've been living in into a realm of positivity and possibility! Your world will become a world in which magic and miracles can happen.

And now, dear brothers and sisters, one final thing. Fix your thoughts on what is true, and honorable, and right, and pure, and lovely, and admirable. Think about things that are excellent and worthy of praise.

-Philippians 4:8

The quickest and easiest example I've heard which shows the power of subliminal programming this:

Think of anything you want, except a pink elephant!

You see what I'm getting at and I'm pretty sure I know what you were just thinking about.

Programming Throughout History: Rituals

Throughout history, and even today, some of the most successful individuals and groups of people have used rituals to help them achieve their goals. You will find rituals in almost every known human society that has ever existed. The Mayans, the Egyptians, the Native Americans, the Americans, the Mexicans, the Japanese, the Christians, the Muslims, the Jewish, the United States government and the Freemasons just scratch the surface of groups of people with significant rituals.

Some rituals seem silly and others can be quite serious. Some rituals make sense while others make you wonder. Some are performed so commonly that we don't even think of them as rituals: marriages, funerals, the presidential inauguration, fraternity and sorority rush, saying "bless you" after someone sneezes, graduations. Even shaking hands, a ritual humans have been doing since the 5th century BC, is something we do every time we meet someone to convey trust and equality. Ever hear about human sacrifices or animal sacrifices to get in good favor with God? If you're Catholic, you've seen the lighting of a candle in church as a contribution to the saints to get in their good favor. There's the initiation ceremony of confirmation which involves the "laying on of hands" and anointing for the purpose of bestowing the gifts of the Holy Spirit. Is that magic? Is that voodoo? Some would say yes, but many others believe that it is necessary to reach a desired end. The list of rituals is endless.

If I told you that you could help yourself in achieving your goal if you poured water over your head, would you think I'm crazy? This ritual has been used in Christianity for centuries and is still used today. Most Christians feel that baptism, a ritual symbolizing the cleansing of sins and the union with Christ so that the believer may be what that faith calls "saved" or "born again", is neces-sary for salvation. Jesus himself was baptized in a river by a man named John.

The point is that rituals help us materialize certain ideals and manifest certain goals we wish to accomplish. Humans have been using ritualistic methods for centuries to get closer to God.

So why not religiously use rituals to get you closer to your goals? You won't be trying to achieve God, you will only be try-ing to get that job, ace that exam, decrease that debt or lose that weight.

If programming is real, and if powerful organizations and soci-eties have been using rituals for thousands of years, would it not behoove us to start programming our Minds with the programs we want to have running up there? We need to "make an offering to the gods" every day. You must create rituals that will condition you to be able to achieve your goals. Even if contributing daily to your mission seems bogus, it gives you psychological power, which brings us back to the point that perception is everything. If you know that you are contributing daily to the execution of your goals and to this "higher power" (whatever that may be to you), you will give yourself a mental edge.

Rituals help to convince yourself that you are capable of being what you desire to be. You are preparing yourself. You are seducing, convincing, inducing, urging, prompting, swaying, enticing, coaxing and cajoling yourself into simply believing that you can do or be something.

One of the purposes of a ritual is to satisfy the spiritual or emotional need of the person performing it. When you have a certain need, specifically a goal, the task of reaching that goal is made easier when preceded by a mapped out plan with structured rituals. These rituals help aid in materializing the desires you hold in your mind as mental pictures.

We must learn to regain control of our thoughts. We must learn to take care of our Minds. We must realize that we are in control of what goes into our mainframe, the master computer. Remember, the powerful mighty Force within only acts and performs according to the thoughts that You give it or that You allow to creep in through your five senses.

The Powerful Subconscious will not do anything other than what you tell it to do. It will only accept the words, images and philosophies that you subject it to. Think of it as a memory card that will download and remember every sight and sound that you allow to reach it. Our daily aim should be to completely eradicate and exterminate from our mental realm any negative, debilitating, crippling thoughts and replace them with everything we desire.

See it and believe it to see it and conceive it

If subliminal messaging and programming is real, and images can strongly influence our thought patterns and behavior, shouldn't we use this secret knowledge to program ourSelves to be the type of person we want to be? Isn't that much better than being subject to what others want us to be?

I used this knowledge in 2001 while in college and training to get drafted into the NFL. Making it to the NFL was my aim and I was working incredibly hard at it. I used as motivation a picture of Kyle Brady who is from my hometown and went to my high school, Cedar Cliff. He had been drafted years earlier in the first round of the NFL draft. I saw him in that picture, up on stage in New York City with my head coach of Cedar Cliff, the legendary Bob Craig, and it was all the motivation I needed.

Every time I caught a glimpse of that picture my pains subsided. The stress, strain and struggle of the hard work was worth it. I knew that I could do it too. I wanted that constant reminder and motivation so I put it above my bed and as I went to sleep every night it was the last thing I saw and the first thing I saw every morning. My roommates thought I was crazy and would always ask me if I would rather have a picture of a naked girl up there. I just told them that I had other things on my mind.

I have used that technique often over the years. The term "Vision Board" became popular when the technique was used in the movie version of the book "The Secret". I like the concept of the Vision Board because it's an actual physical board. All you need is a 36x24 piece of foam core or any other type of bulletin board type material. Cut out or print pictures and images of all the things you want to have in your life. Maybe there is a picture of the type of car you want to drive. Maybe one picture could be the house you want to have some day in your life. Maybe another picture could be the beach destination you want to travel to this year. You can also print out a specific goal (top salesman in the company, the number of sales you want to make, the number of new clients you want to sign, the amount of money you want to see in your bank account, the number of homeruns you want to hit, goals you want to score or the time you want to swim) on paper and affix it to the Vision Board.

Once you create this Vision Board you need to put it somewhere you'll see it every day. Ideally it should be like my photo of Kyle Brady, in a place where you see it last thing at night and first thing in the morning.

Your Vision Board should be something you glance at for a few minutes each day to visually program your mind for the things you want to happen in your life. Seeing your desires every day helps to summon up all the forces that are within you that will enable you to achieve them. We must constantly tantalize ourselves and entice our appetites if we are ever to taste what we yearn for. We have to actively seduce ourselves with images that will draw us closer to our cravings. With your Vision Board and its programing you are calling upon the energy inside of you to allow yourself to take what is yours, your life's desires. You are more Powerful than You know.

The mind is like an iceberg, It floats with one-seventh of its bulk above water.

— Sigmund Freud

GOAL
SETTING

Flow Like Water

If you've ever stopped to look at a brook or a stream, you have noticed that as long as the water flows towards its goal (which is the ocean), and as long as it has good movement, the water is fresh and sparkling and alive. But sometimes along the bank of the brook or stream there will be a pocket of water that becomes trapped off to the side. The trapped water is cut off from the rest of the moving water and has stopped progressing downstream towards its goal. This trapped water becomes a stagnant pool. The water trapped there becomes very dark and murky and mold, mildew and decay set in. Dis-ease sets in.

It's also this way with human lives. If people stop setting goals and cease to aspire, and they stop moving towards something greater than themselves, they begin to decay. If they stop moving and progressing towards their goals their lives become stagnant. When this happens to someone it means they have become content with living a boring and monotonous life with no purpose. Essentially they begin to rot mentally, physically, and spiritually. They may begin to feel uneasy even though they enjoy the "comfort" of being content and lazy. In some cases, because there is no movement and progress in their life, dis-ease sets in. Their body may actually develop some sort of physical disease or illness. They may become depressed or irritable because, like the stream, parts of them have become stagnant. They stagnate and they begin to wilt away because there is no movement or flow to their life. The secret to life, in all of nature and in all of creation, is movement. Never be content.

We must learn to commit ourselves to a lifetime of movement, development and progress. It's sometimes slow, but it is steady and it always leads to growth.

No matter how young, old, happy or sad we become, we must never stop setting goals. We must always have aspirations and goals which propel us towards progress, growth and a life ultimately full of greatness.

The average length of the career of a NFL football player is only three years and there are many reasons for this. For most of their lives, the young football player's dream and goal in life is to make it to the NFL. They have a clear-cut vision of what they want, and with a laser-like focus, extreme dedication and discipline they pursue their goal. They rise up every day to be the best version of themselves they can possibly be. Finally, after all those years of dedication, determination and perseverance, if fortunate enough, the football player makes it to the NFL.

When they make it, however, a majority begin to develop the attitude that they have arrived. They begin to rest on their laurels. Sure, they may continue to work hard, but because they "made it", maybe they don't work quite as hard as they once did. Maybe they aren't quite as hungry as they used to be. Maybe they start staying out a little later than they used to. Maybe they start drinking a little more, partying a little more and spending time with more girls than they used to. They start "living the life" a little more because they feel they deserve it since they've arrived and made it to the destination they've been seeking their entire football-playing lives. That's the whole problem: simply reaching the NFL was their goal.

Sooner than later, a player doesn't quite have the same passion that he once had. He doesn't have the same hunger and FIRE he once had. And what happens? He gets FIRED.

The reason the average career is only three years is because a majority of the players who make it forget to set new goals once in the NFL. Once they've achieved the goal they've always worked towards, they forget to set new goals to drive them and allow them to continue to progress and get better. With no new goals in their life their lives become stagnant and, like the stream, they slowly begin to rot and decay. Eventually all that remains is the empty shell of the purpose-driven Force of energy they once were.

I have found that the players who last in the NFL, the players who are blessed enough to last longer than the average, are those who are never content. The players who play five, seven or nine years or more, are those who are constantly striving to be better. They do everything they can to get a little better each day. Whether it's studying extra film of the opponent, spending extra time in the weight room or on the practice field fine-tuning their skills, the true pros always strive to get better and they always have specific goals in mind. After numerous Probowls and a guaranteed Hall of Fame induction, I watched my friend Tony Gonzalez go out to practice early every day to catch passes. Tony has the Mind of a

Champion. He's never content.

True champions know exactly what it is they want to do, and because they have that clear-cut vision of what they want to do in life, it is easier for them to know all the things that need to be done to help them get there. Because of this they keep moving. They keep progressing towards their destination. They flow like water.

Never Be Content

I love setting goals for myself because I love the feeling of achieving them even more. Sometimes people ask me how I was able to make it in the NFL for nine years. The conclusion that I've come to regarding my longevity is that I'm always striving to be better. I have never let myself become content. Every time I've accomplished something that I've set out to achieve I have immediately re-established a new goal for my life. Everytime I accomplish one of my goals, I immediately set a new one and prepare myself to work harder than I ever have before. Well, ok I admit, maybe I take a little time off to enjoy the fruits of my mental labor.

I never want to be content or feel like I've "arrived" because the moment I do I know I will have lost my edge. When that happens, someone with more passion and drive will pass me by. Each day I wake up and my hope is that I can be a little better that day than I was the day before. I want to be better at everything I do. I want to walk better and talk better. I want to be better at drinking and eating, breathing and sleeping. I want to be better at loving and hugging, laughing and having fun. I want to be a better friend, husband, brother and son.

When you don't set goals there is no real movement or growth toward anything that will bring lasting happiness. The old saying, "Idle hands are the devil's workshop" is so true. If you sit around doing nothing because you have no goals in life, and if you stop working towards or pursuing your goals, bad things start to happen.

Many people have given up setting goals for themselves. When that happens they've basically given up on their hopes and dreams, and they have stopped aspiring to become more than they already are. They become content with life and have stopped progressing. Because there is no real excitement or sense of purpose in their life, they try to bring excitement into it by turning to frivolous outlets like watching TV, drinking, doing drugs and partying, and even creating drama out of the simplest situations just so they have something TO DO.

Most high school students in our country, although they go to school, are not educating themselves. They just go through the motions. Sure they show up to class, but they just do it because it's what they have to do. High school graduation rates in our country are disheartening. Are classes getting more difficult? Genetically, is our youth getting dumber? No, and no. Kids are just not trying hard enough. They have no motivation to excel in the classroom because they don't have real goals for their lives. If they have to go to class and sit there listening to the teacher, they might as well pay attention and get good grades, right? Wrong. That is not how they see it.

Today's youth isn't the only demographic with a lack of motivation. Many working adults in our country today are caught up in the rat race. They are working a job that they don't really enjoy, plodding through the daily grind of their job, counting the hours until they get to go home. There is no real passion and no sense of purpose to what they do. We all know someone whose work has become a monotonous and boring ritual. They do it because they have conditioned themselves to think that it is the norm for people to spend their entire lives making enough money just so they can retire. At that point they feel that they will finally be able to "enjoy" life and do all the things they've always wanted to do. It is then that they will finally live the life they always wanted to live, right? Wrong.

What happens to these people that make up the majority in our country? What happens to these people who just run the rat race and go through the motions with no real focus, passion, direction and goals? They work and they work and waste their days just making money at a boring job they're not emotionally connected to. Before they know it, 25 years of their life have flown by and they realize they are too old and too tired to enjoy life the way they thought they would. They were in such a zombie-like daze that half their life passed them by and they didn't get anywhere!

People who once had grand plans to travel the world when they retired often never end up taking the trips they had planned because they have become too old and too tired. So instead, they end up sitting at home bored. All that work that was so tiresome really did enable them to RE-tire, to simply get tired and bored all over again.

If only they had set goals for themselves along the way, goals that would challenge them and motivate them every day. If they'd done that they would have been able to wake up each morning with a sense of purpose and passion about what they were doing with their lives. Their lives would have stayed fresh, lively and exciting. They would have been making consistent and gradual progress and over the course of many years they really would have made great strides in life. After 25 years of their life passed by, they could have looked back and said, "Wow! I have lived a wonderful life! I've done so much, and I've seen so much!" They would not have had as many regrets because they actually lived. They would not have lived life as a robot, going through the motions.

I'm not saying you should quit your job if your work life is boring and monotonous. No matter what job we have, no matter where we go to school, no matter what we do, we can always set goals for ourselves. We can always strive to be better. Even if the goal is to make four other people at the office smile today, we can always set goals that will improve the quality of our life and the lives of those around us. What we must aim for is gradual progress. In certain Asian cultures, they have a saying:

If you see a characteristic in another person that you admire or respect, you should adopt that characteristic and try to emulate it and make it work for you in your own life. If you see something in another that bothers you, rid yourself of anything in you that may resemble the negative quality that you dislike.

When we start looking at life in this way, our lives will change forever. We start making gradual progress each and every day. We will see each and every day, each and every moment, as an opportunity to do one of three things: Get better, get worse or stay the same. The person we are now is a result of all the decisions and progress we have made.

One of your main aims in life should be to be a little better today than you were yesterday.

That is it. Sounds simple, right? If we are able to grow in this manner, just a little bit better each day, years from now you will be able to look back at your life and see the progress you've made. To be able to see that is a wonderful feeling.

If you continue to do this throughout your life you allow yourself to make gradual progress and you will continuously refine yourself.

Picture your life as a garden. If you continually plant good seeds, you will see healthy growth. The good plants will produce delicious fruits that will nourish you and give you strength and energy. You must nurture the healthy plants in your garden and tend to them so they continue to grow healthy and strong. If you become content, weeds and insects will appear in the garden. These intruders are harmful and You must constantly work to rid your garden of these negative influences.

If they are not removed, all of the good and healthy aspects and the future of your garden will be intruded upon, pushed to the side, overshadowed and, worst of all, they may be eaten away and die off completely. Our lives are the same as the garden. We must continue to plant positive seeds and set new goals in our life. We must continually tend to our gardens, and constantly work to make progress in our lives. This approach allows for gradual progress. Never be content.

Get Off the Treadmill! Set Lofty Goals

There is a disease in our country that has been running rampant for quite some time. It is growing stronger and stronger and an increasing number of people are losing their lives to this disease every day. People in positions of power know about this disease and many of them do not want the masses to realize that this epidemic is spreading. They want the masses to catch this disease and spread it so that they themselves can remain at the top of the food chain. They do not want the people to know that they can conquer this crippling disease. They don't want them to know they possess the cure and can remedy the problem, becoming elite leaders and champions themselves. The disease is called the Treadmill Syndrome. It's a condition in which a person, due to a lack of motivation or a failure to set goals, makes no progress in life.

Although the person thinks they are doing things in life to better their situation, they are making absolutely no progress.

The people who suffer and lose their lives to this disease are the millions of people who don't realize that they need to set lofty goals in life if they are ever going to make any real progress and reach their full potential. The millions of people in our country who have not set lofty goals are like a person running on a tread-mill. They run and they run, and they work and they work, but they go absolutely nowhere.

The people who spend year after year in the same position without any upward movement have Treadmill Syndrome. The people who say they want to be a great athlete but only do the same amount of work that everyone else does have Treadmill Syndrome. The people who say they want to lose weight but exercise only occasionally and don't consistently adhere to a strict diet have Treadmill Syndrome. The people who say they want to be one of the top performers in their company but they only do the minimum job requirement have Treadmill Syndrome. These are some examples of the types of people who work and work all their lives but never really get anywhere.

If you don't set lofty goals in life, you will waste away your days and, regardless of how hard you work you will never reach your full potential.

If you don't challenge yourself with lofty goals that force you to move beyond your current circumstance, your life will become like stagnant water. In the blink of an eye your life will pass you by and you will not have accomplished a fraction of what you would've, could've and should've.

When you take the time to study yourself, and know what you really want in life, you will then be able to set lofty goals that will propel you towards the things you want. You will be able to get off the treadmill and start making real strides in your life. Each step you take will bring you closer to the proximity of your goals. Finally, you will be able to make real progress and actually go places with your life.

If you know who you are, what you want and what you are capable of, then you will know what you must do to become all that you are meant to be. Stop being content. Set massive goals for your life. Start pursuing your goals with a relentless passion.

Do You Set Realistic Goals?

Setting realistic goals is one of the most vital keys to achieving the success that you are meant to achieve. Earlier in the book, I asked "Do you know your Self?" Knowing thyself is an essential component of setting realistic goals because only after discovering who you really are (the specific talents, gifts, and passions you possess) will you be able to pursue what you are meant to do. Otherwise, everything you do will be in vain. Often, you see people chasing dreams and goals that just aren't right for them. I think the main reason for this is that people look at others who have already achieved success and think what works for others could work for them. When they think this they actually want to be that other person, which is the central mistake.

As soon as you want to be someone other than the Great You, you become a phony, an imitation. You become like that bowl of plastic fruit that looks good at first, but when you really get to know it you realize that it's only an imitation. Rather than looking at the person in the mirror and realizing the greatness that reflection possesses, and accepting the unique path they are meant to travel, they look to others and try to augment their life to be like that of someone else who has already achieved their greatness. You must realize that people who have achieved success have walked the path that was meant for them. That's why they are special. They are special because they know who they are and they are good at being themselves!

When you are good at being yourself, you are special. You are unique. You are unlike any other person that has ever walked this Earth. When you become good at being You, others will realize that there is no one in the world like you.

I'm not saying that you shouldn't look to others to learn, or that you shouldn't adopt certain ways of doings things from those who have achieved success because that is the exact the purpose of this book. What I'm saying is that although you will learn from others and use their experiences and examples to make you better, you must never forget that you are not those other people. You are unique.

You are special and original, and the moment you lose the uniqueness that makes you that way, you become a clone. As T.D. Jakes once said, "You become a cheap copy of a great original."

You must not lose You in your search for greatness. Always remember who you are and from where you have come. Always remember all the unique qualities that make you an original. Being an original gives you an edge. Yes, find out what has made others great and use that knowledge to improve yourself and do those things which will make the Original You better, but don't try to be someone else, just be you.

What happens when you do not set realistic goals? In psychology there is the concept of Cognitive Dissonance, an uncomfortable feeling caused by holding two contradictory ideas simultaneously. If you don't set realistic and attainable goals you will experience Cognitive Dissonance and you will feel uncomfortable. You may say you want to achieve a goal but if it's not realistic and attainable, deep down you will know, and you will get that uncomfortable feeling.

> "Most children grow up with dreams of being the next Michael
> Jordan, Florence Griffith-Joyner, Emmit Smith, Monica Seles,
> or Mark McGwire. But in reality, less than 1/10th of 1% of
> high school athletes ever come close to reaching this level.
> Nevertheless, there is nothing wrong with having dreams.
> But when the time comes to choose a college and compete at
> the collegiate level, our children must be honest and realistic about their talent and abilities. We can't allow them to
> set the chin bar so high that they could never reach it. Some
> examples would be: a 5'2" basketball player that wants to go
> to North Carolina to play basketball, or an offensive lineman
> that is 5'8" – 210 lbs. that wants to play for Notre Dame, or
> even a female soccer player that runs a 7.3 – 40 yard dash
> that wants to play for the University of Texas. I believe that
> the first critical step our children take in considering college
> athletics is evaluating their own talent level and setting attainable goals."
>
> -The Student-Athlete & College Recruiting

As revealed in Evaluate Yourself in Chapter 2, we must know

who we are. We must evaluate ourselves so that we reduce our chances of experiencing Cognitive Dissonance. Being able to recognize and acknowledge this "uncomfortable feeling" is a skill that can and must be fine-tuned if we are ever to truly know ourselves. We are all equipped with innate tools that help us know what is right and what is not. Many people take these tools for granted and do not even know that they are there to begin with. Sometimes their lives are too busy and hectic to ever even notice them. We must all be still and know what is right for us.

Why do you think monks meditate for hours on end? Why do you think at almost every pivotal moment in the Bible, Jesus "went off by himself to the mountains to meditate?"

The truly wise know that it is vital that one listens to that still, small voice within. The sages, magi and shaman all know that one of the greatest secrets in life is to Know Thyself. We must constantly perform self-analysis. We must consistently study ourselves and listen to the wisdom within. The Captain within our Soul wants to steer our ships toward greatness and we must learn to listen to its directions. If we lie to ourselves about who we really are, we are cheating ourselves and inevitably we will experience Cognitive Dissonance. One of the greatest men I have ever known is my wrestling and football coach at Cedar Cliff High School, Bob Craig. He had this quote on the back of his business card:

You may fool the whole world down
the pathway of years,
and get pats on the back as you pass,
but your final reward will be
heartache and tears
if you've cheated the man in the glass.

-Dale Wimbrow

We have to be realistic about the goals we set, but also know that what is realistic for each of us is determined by none other than ourselves. It's like in the movie "The Matrix" when the main character, Neo, goes to see the Oracle who is to tell him his destiny. Essentially, Neo wants to know whether or not he is the One who can save the people. Their exchange goes like this:

The Oracle: You know why Morpheus brought you to see me?

Neo: I think so.

The Oracle: So, what do you think? Do you think you're The One?

Neo: I don't know.

The Oracle: You know what that means? (She points to a sign on the wall) It's Latin. Means 'Know thyself'. I'm going to let you in on a little secret. Being The One is just like being in love. No one can tell you you're in love, you just know it. Through and through. Balls to bones.

The Oracle: Well, I better have a look at you. Open your mouth, say Ahhh.

Neo: Ahhh.

The Oracle: Okay. Now I'm supposed to say, `Umm, that's interesting, but...,' then you say...

Neo: But what?

The Oracle: But you already know what I'm going to tell you.

Neo: I'm not The One.

The Oracle: Sorry, kid. You got the gift, but it looks like you're waiting for something.

Neo: What?

The Oracle: Your next life maybe, who knows? That's the way these things go.

The Oracle let Neo say what he believed in his own mind and knew that as he believed, so it would be. The funny thing is, if Neo had said "I am the one," The Oracle would have said "Yep you're right. You da man!"

In order to set realistic goals for ourselves, we must know who we are and of what we are capable. We alone decide what is and is not possible in our lives. But in order to live in Peace, we must be honest with ourselves. We must neither cheat ourselves nor lie to ourselves. We must be true to ourselves. We must be realistic about the goals we choose to set for ourselves.

How To Set Realistic Goals

Ok, so some you may be wondering how you actually can know yourSelf and how to know if your goals are actually realistic. Well, believe it or not, the first step is really easy! It's easy because good ol' Mother Nature has put within each of us a barometer which measures the "rightness" or "wrongness" of our beliefs.

We all have had those little hairs on the back of our neck stand up when we were faced with a dangerous situation or that "gut feeling" that told you which way to turn when you were trying to find the aisle with the peanut butter. Surely you've had the "butterflies" when you met that special someone who made your heart jump up into your throat.

So, you see, there is plenty of evidence that the Innate Intelligence which resides within each of us will not steer us wrong if we make a pointed effort to notice it. Eckhart Tolle explains this concept in his book "The Power of Now". When you take some time out of your busy day to meditate and know thyself, to truly contemplate who you are and what you are meant to do, the answer will be given to you. When this answer is given to you, you will know it. You will get very excited about what you want to do. It will be a gut feeling. You may even say it out loud. You'll fearlessly tell yourSelf this is what you were meant to do. It's what you were born to do.

Considered by many as the most popular spiritual author in the United States, Eckhart Tolle underwent a transformation at 29 that influenced "The Power of Now", a book that has sold over three million copies.

You will know when you discover what it is you are meant to do. You will get a gut feeling. You'll just know and feel it. Once you know who you are and what you are meant to do, you will then be able to set attainable, realistic and specific goals. As I mentioned earlier, it is vital that we continually perform self-analysis. Self-reflection is the best way to know thyself.

The doubter in all of us will cause us to be apprehensive about getting that gut feeling and being able to recognize it. Seeking innate wisdom will remove this apprehension and deliver both the gut feeling and our abilities of recognition.

For everyone who asks, receives.
Everyone who seeks, finds.
And to everyone who knocks,
the door will be opened.

–Matthew 7:8

If you have not yet discovered who you are and what you are meant to do, you will if you seek it diligently. This process of self-discovery often takes time. Rarely does someone know exactly what it is that they are meant to do from the time they are young. Most people have to dig deep to find that which they are destined to do. If you have been seeking but have not yet found exactly what it is you seek, at the very least you will discover things about yourself that you needed to know. You may not discover what you are meant to do, but you may find out what you are not meant to do. That is just as important!

You will discover things in your life that you find more interesting and appealing than others. There will surely be certain things that interest you and intrigue you. When you discover interests and avenues that you could see yourself pursuing, pick the thing that speaks to you most. Pick that path that calls out to you most and go for it. Even if you eventually find out that it was not what you were really meant to do, it is better to have gone for something and made progress than to have made none. Stay away from the Treadmill Syndrome. When you pick a goal and go for it, you make progress, you learn from your experiences and mistakes, you grow and you develop character and skills along the way that will surely benefit you in the future when you do find what you are meant to do. Do not shy away from the process of self-discovery. Embrace it.

Our deepest fear is not that we are inadequate. Our deepest fear is that we are powerful beyond measure. It is our light, not our darkness that most frightens us. We ask ourselves, "Who am I to be brilliant, gorgeous, talented, and fabulous?" Actually, who are you not to be? You are a child of God. Your playing small doesn't serve the world. There's nothing enlightened about shrinking so that other people won't feel insecure around you. We were born to make manifest the glory of God that is within us. It's not just in some of us, it's in everyone. And as we let our own light shine, we unconsciously give others permission to do the same. As we are liberated from our own fear, our presence automatically liberates others.

-Nelson Mandela, 1994

Set an Ultimate Goal

What is your ultimate goal? How does one set an ultimate goal? This is a discerning task and we have to be very calculated when setting an ultimate goal for ourselves. Our ultimate goal cannot be an aspiration we set so high that we cannot ever convince ourselves that we could actually achieve it. It has to be believable. It cannot be set so low that it is easily attained and we sell ourselves short. If the goal is too easily attained, then we probably had more fuel in the tank and could have achieved more. The other thing we must not do is set our sights directly on what we want. It has to be just above what we want. We have to think about what we want and then set our sights just above that. If you reach for the stars and fall short at least you're still landing on the moon.

We also must dream big when we set our ultimate goal. This is the goal that really makes us reach. This is the goal that if we were to achieve it, it would be like a dream come true. Set your sights high. This is not where you set small goals. We will do that in the next section when we talk about stepping-stone goals. This is where we do the big thinking. This has to be the goal that makes us say to ourselves, "Someone's going to do it, why not me?" Set an Ultimate Goal.

I am extremely thankful for one of the most inspiring coaches I have ever had, Bobby April. Bobby shared this story with us when I played for the Buffalo Bills. It is a story about setting ultimate goals, dreaming big and believing in yourself:

> *Back in the 1930's and 1940's runners in track and field were steadily approaching the four-minute mile landmark. In 1945 Gunder Hägg of Sweden broke the world record by running the mile in 4:01.4. And then all progress came to a standstill. Nobody could break the record time that Gunder had set. For nine years the record stood strong and people began to believe that the record would never be broken, that humans had reached their full potential and the four-minute mile would never be broken. Along comes Roger Bannister. Roger Bannister set a goal. He was determined to break the record and run a sub four-minute mile. With incredible vision, belief in himself and a very specific goal in mind, Bannister pushed on despite what everyone said. On May 6th 1954, Roger Bannister broke the four-minute mile by running a 3:59.4 at Iffley Road Track in Oxford. And do you want to know how crazy the human mind is? When that barrier that was thought to be impossible to break was broken, within six weeks another man ran a sub four-minute mile! A record that stood for nine years was broken and within six weeks someone else broke it! Over the course of the next 18 months, seven others ran a sub four-minute mile!*

So, you see, we must have great vision for our life. We must think beyond what others may tell us we should be or become. We need to think about how great we want to be and we must go for it. We must set an ultimate goal for our life. Once we know where we want to go, it is much easier to set up a plan and create a blueprint for our success.

Set Stepping-Stone Goals

"The journey of a thousand miles begins with a single step"

— Lao Tzu

Many never accomplish the grand plans that they once had for their lives. Countless people never realize their dreams and aspirations. Is it because they fell short? Is it because they didn't possess the skill or talent? Is it because they didn't persevere and finish the work? NO! As crazy as it may sound, most people don't even start working towards their goals!

Often, people who have lofty goals and expectations never even try to achieve them because they don't think there is ever a chance that they can. They see the huge goal and they are frightened by the thought of it. Their goal seems unachievable. The mountain looks too high to climb. They think they'll never be to accomplish their goal. People often lose before the race even begins.

It's good to have an end goal in mind, but that isn't what we must focus on. We must focus on much smaller, more tangible goals that will bring us closer to achieving the ultimate goal. Baby steps are the way. When you make gradual progress each and every day, that ultimate goal will look more attainable every time you look up at it. After days, months or years of daily, gradual progress you will look back and see how far you've come. You may even do more than you had originally set out to achieve.

I have a saying that embodies this idea: Daily, gradual progress garners gargantuan results.

When I was a freshman in high school I was a pretty good wrestler. Even though I was wrestling juniors and seniors, I was winning. That year I was having a phenomenal season and so was our entire team. We were one of the best in the area. Nine days before we were going to wrestle our rivals, the Cumberland Valley Eagles who, at the time, was the best team in our conference, I had some bad luck.

I was really looking forward to the big matchup. One day at practice while preparing misfortune struck. I was wrestling with my teammate and I felt my knee pop. It hurt pretty badly and I knew right away that something wasn't right. I tried to straighten out my leg but I couldn't. As I lay on the mat, writhing in pain with my coaches and teammates hovered over me, all I thought about was, "Not now! No! God, please, no! Don't let me be hurt right now!"

I was taken to the hospital and after X-Rays and an MRI; I found out that I had torn cartilage in my knee. Part of my medial meniscus had torn away and was jammed in my knee joint in a way that wouldn't allow me to straighten my leg. I was told that I needed surgery. I asked the doctor how long I would be out and he said that usually it takes two or maybe three weeks before one can ease back into normal activity.

"But Doc", I said, "I have to wrestle against Cumberland Valley! It's the biggest match of the year."

"Well, ok Coy, when is the match? ", he asked.

"It's in seven days Doc and I can't miss it," I insisted.

"Easy there buddy, not so fast", said the Doc shaking his head. "You're probably not going to be able to wrestle in that match. You're going to be in some pain for a while after the surgery. I'm thinking you'll need two weeks or more to recover."

I became silent and I said nothing else. The doctor said he had to go check his schedule so we could set up a surgery time and he left the room. Inside my head I started smiling because I had heard all that I needed to hear. He said that I "probably" wasn't going to be able to wrestle in that match. He didn't say that I was definitely going to miss that match. I knew in that moment that there was a chance I could make it back. He gave me a little glimmer of hope and that's all I needed. I knew that I could wrestle in that match and help my team win.

As soon as the doctor left the room I told my parents, who were in the room with me, how badly I wanted to wrestle in that big matchup. I told them that I believed I would be able to recover from surgery faster than anyone, and I could bear the pain. My parents had great hesitation and concern, as any parent would, but they knew how much this match meant to me.

Thank God for my parents. They have always been the epitome of support and love. They said that by some miracle if I was able to heal quickly enough for the match and if the doctor said that my knee would be structurally fine, gave me the green light and I was willing to deal with the pain, they would support me.

When the doctor came back in the room, my parents asked if he thought it would be possible, if I were to heal very quickly, for me to wrestle seven days later. The doctor told them that after the cartilage was removed, the knee would be fine structurally, but there would be a lot of swelling and pain. He said that he highly doubted I would be able to wrestle seven days later, but that if I was able to deal with the pain, he would examine me and consider allowing it. Right then it was on and I knew I could do it.

I had the surgery exactly seven days before the big match. The doctor said that everything had gone extremely well and that now it was just a matter of time. My parents drove me home after the surgery, and as I hobbled into the house on crutches, I began to have a different outlook about my ultimate goal of wrestling seven days later.

Before the surgery, although it seemed like an aggressive and lofty goal, I felt that I would be able to achieve it with no problem. After the surgery, however, when all the pain and swelling set in, my goal began to seem far-fetched and even unattainable. What in the world was I thinking? Seven days later? Wrestle in the biggest match of the year after a knee surgery against a strong and completely healthy opponent?

"I must have been crazy," I thought to myself. My knee was so swollen and it hurt so badly. I looked at the stitches and began to think that I should just give up on my ultimate goal of wrestling seven days later. Being that it was such a lofty goal, I almost gave up on it before I even started tying to achieve that goal. I almost didn't even give myself a chance.

My parents could see how badly I wanted to wrestle and they didn't want me to see me give up so they explained to me that I needed to set small goals first. They said that although I needed to have my ultimate goal in mind, I needed to put that in the back of my mind and focus first on smaller, more easily attainable stepping-stone goals. I needed to give myself little goals that were easier to accomplish and with every stepping-stone goal I achieved, my ultimate goal would be one step closer. They explained that if we focus only on the ultimate goal it could prove to be overwhelming and seemingly impossible to achieve.

They explained how anything you wish to accomplish in life must be conquered in steps. You must crawl before you can wall and walk before you can run (or wrestle). They knew that if I set stepping-stone goals for myself I would slowly build the confidence that I needed to reach my ultimate goal. If I approached my goal in that way, they explained, even if I didn't end up achieving that ultimate goal, I would be at peace about it because I had gone after my goal and made progress and I would have done everything that I could've to try to achieve that goal. I understood and we began setting stepping-stone goals for my recovery. I didn't have to be ready to wrestle against Cumberland Valley now. My ultimate goal was seven days away. I had seven whole days to prepare myself and be ready to accomplish that goal.

I needed to start small. My first goal was going to be a simple task, just being able to bend the knee. One small stepping-stone goal at a time, I started the plan that would possibly afford me the opportunity of achieving my ultimate goal.

The first couple of days, I could only bend my knee slightly. It hurt pretty badly but I kept focusing on that task. I continued to work and eventually I became more comfortable with bending it a little more. Then my goal was to straighten my knee completely. That hurt badly too, but I kept focusing on that little task and was eventually able to straighten it more. Although I was not yet bending or straightening it completely, I added the next task of standing without my crutches by the end of day three. I had to begin to put weight on my knee if I was going to continue to make progress and give myself a chance of reaching my goal. By the end of the fourth day I was able to bend and straighten it almost completely. I was also able to put a little bit of weight on it without crutches. Although the tasks were painful and the progress seemed slow, I was doing all the necessary steps.

Day five was the day that it was time to really push myself. If I was going to wrestle on the seventh day, I really needed to be able to walk on it and put my weight on that knee on the fifth day. That day and its tasks was a critical stepping-stone goal. It would be the goal that determined whether or not the ultimate goal was even an option. I went to work. I tried walking on that knee and tried doing squats. Although I was able to do it ever so slowly and carefully, those muscles around the knee just didn't want to fire completely because they were turned off. Those muscles just wanted to rest and didn't want to have to work because they had just been cut and intruded upon. I had to make them work.

That day went well. At the end of a good day of progress, despite being able to walk normally and squat completely, my parents and I knew that the next day, day six, was going to be the biggest test of all.

On day six I woke up and looked down at my knee and said, "Well, let's see what you can do buddy." My dad told me that he wanted to take me somewhere. He was going to take me to a place where we could test the knee to see if it was going to be ready to go the next day. I was walking with only a slight limp as we approached the car, and I wondered where he was going to take me. Was he going to take me to the wrestling gym? Had he called one of my teammates to wrestle with me?

My dad looked over at me before we started to drive, and he told me that we were going to go to Hershey Park Arena.

"Why," I asked.

"There are a lot of stadium steps in there, Coy," my dad explained. "If you can climb those steps, then maybe that will be a sign as to whether you will be ready to go tomorrow. We are going to walk up those steps together."

When we got inside the arena, the sight of the stadium steps was quite imposing. There had to be over one hundred steps to the top. My dad said, "Alright, Coy, let's do this one step at a time."

It seemed like the throbbing in my knee began at the thought of climbing those stairs. What was I thinking? All the pain made me begin to feel as if I was not going to be able to do it. My goal was to conquer one step at a time. That was it, just one step at a time. I took the first step and despite the pain, I pushed through it. One step, down, but then another and another. The seemingly impossible goal of wrestling seven days later that I had set for myself began to seem a little more achievable and realistic with every stepping-stone goal. With every literal step that I took up those stadium steps, my confidence grew. With each step I got a little stronger, and the task easier. I could feel my muscles starting to fire more completely and fully.

I started moving up more quickly and the pain seemed to fade. My hope heated up from a small kindling until I began to feel a flame burning within. I made it all the way to the top with my dad beside me every step of the way, and I remember crying when we made it to the top. I was so happy. I was so thankful that my parents had taught me about setting smaller goals that eventually lead to the ultimate goal. I had accomplished my stepping-stone goals. I knew that I had prepared myself mentally for the challenge. I knew in that moment that my ultimate goal was achievable. Wrestling the next day was possible.

Looking back on that day, I am so thankful for my dad's genius. Our house had plenty of stairs. We had a basement with a flight of stairs and our house had a second story with a flight of stairs which led up to the bedrooms. I realize now that, more than anything, my dad wanted to test my mind that day. He knew that if I was able to look at an empty stadium full of intimidating steps that seemed to climb forever and I was still willing to go for it then maybe I was ready. I remember thinking how those stadium steps represented all the steps that had led me to that pivotal moment which would determine whether or not I would reach my goal. I thought about how with each step that I was able to take, I

COY WIRE • WWW.COYWIRE.COM

was one step closer to my ultimate goal. The valuable lesson learned through that experience was that the ultimate goals in life are important, but the stepping-stone goals are equally important because they make the Ultimate Goal more tangible and attainable.

By the way, only seven days after surgery, I won that match against Cumberland Valley. Boom.

If my parents had not helped me set stepping-stone goals the previous days and I had gone out and tried to wrestle immediately, I would have never made it. The Ultimate Goal would have seemed too grand. So many people have had great dreams and aspirations but they never even started the journey because it seemed too tough of a task. The mountain looked too high to climb.

Climbers who trek Mt. Everest understand the importance of setting short-term goals. They reach for specific, pertinent and achievable goals that they can strive towards on a daily basis. Short-term goals are vital to one's success. The ongoing process of achieving short-term goals allows one to remain focused on the task at hand without becoming overwhelmed by the enormity of the Ultimate Goal. Short-term goals help climbers stay focused and committed to the ultimate goal of reaching the summit and coming back down alive.

Don't aim for the end goal just yet, because you have to go through all the obstacles along the way. I always kept that in mind. I said to myself, I am going for the top, that is my goal, but I am going to go through it step by step.

From that step, I am going to go on to the next step and so on, all the way to the Hilary Step.

-(Climber 6)
Journal of Excellence – Issue No. 8
Mental Strategies of Elite Mount Everest Climbers
Shaunna Burke and Terry Orlick, University of Ottawa

When reaching for an Ultimate Goal it is crucial that you focus on the stepping-stone goals. If one was aiming to build a great wall, they should not focus on building a great wall, but instead focus on laying down one brick as perfectly as possible. Then after that brick, they can then focus on laying another one brick as perfectly as possible and so on. If this type of focus, dedication and determination persists, it is only a matter of time before you are able to step back and enjoy the fruits of your labor. A great wall will have been laid one brick at a time.

Set Specific Goals

Be specific when setting your goal. Your Mind is very powerful and obedient. It will do whatever you program it to do and nothing more or nothing less. You must be very aware of what you are programming it to do. If your goal is to be a great athlete, how great do you want to be? If you want to be rich, how rich do you want to be? After all, everyone has a different concept of greatness. To you something may be great, but to someone else it might just be good. You have to be very specific. You even have to be specific about when you want to achieve your goal.

The NFL Scouting Combine is an annual event where college football players perform physical and mental tests in front of NFL coaches, general managers and scouts in an effort to be drafted into the professional football league.

When I was getting ready for the NFL Combine I wrote down all of the goals I had for each drill. I would write the specific goal on a post-it note. On many of the notes I wrote the exact time I wanted to run in the 40-yard dash. On many others I wrote the time I wanted to run in the 20-yard shuttle. On many more I wrote the times for the other shuttles, the height for the vertical jump, the distance for the broad jump and the number of repetitions I wanted to bench 225lbs.

I wrote down the specific times, distances and repetitions I wanted to achieve while at the Combine.

I thought long and hard about what was possible for me and what I wanted to achieve. I wrote them down to the hundredth of a second and the very inch. Of course I placed those notes all over my apartment to the point that it was littered with goal-bearing notes. You could barely even see the walls. I put them on the TV so that I couldn't see the TV anymore. I put them on the bathroom mirrors. I put them on doors, in doorways, on the ceiling, in the fridge and on the fridge. I put them everywhere so I would always be reminded of them. I was programming them into my mind.

My Combine performance was a personal success. Within one hundredth of a second of every single time I had written down for the shuttles and 40-yard dash I achieved my goal! My goal was to bench 225lbs 30 times and I got 29! My goal was to jump 40 inches in the vertical jump and I jumped 38.5"! To this day, I am still in the top-10 fastest times ever for three of the different shuttle agility drills! Powerful, amazing things happen when you write down specific goals.

Examples of Specific Goal-Setting:

Good Goal: be a successful salesman
Better: be the number 1 salesman in the company with the most sales this year

Good Goal: to be a great football player
Better Goal: to be the best quarterback in the entire state by my senior year

Good Goal: to be rich
Better Goal: to have $1,000,000 in my bank account by the time I am 32

SECRET #6:

Sweet Dreams

To get your plans to sink in deep, you must implant them when you sleep

Even though earlier in the book I told you to wake up from your unconscious state during your waking hours, the next secret will help you progress while you sleep at night.

The one thing that bothered me a long time ago was that no matter how hard I worked in a day, there was still a huge portion of my time which I never made any progress. There were so many hours that I could have spent progressing, but I spent doing nothing. That time was when I was asleep at night. Six hours or more every night was time wasted that could have been spent getting better. Then I began to wonder if it has to be a complete waste of time. I know sleep is important and I encourage you to sleep, but what if we could get better while we sleep?

I thought about my mantra. There was no doubt that my mantra had been helping me build my Spirit and persona into what I wanted them to be while I was reciting it throughout the day. What if I could say my mantra all through the night while I slept? I would almost double the amount of time I was able to program my mind and direct my Spirit. I realized that even though my conscious mind may slumber while I slept at night, my ears are still there. I don't sleep with ear plugs. I can still hear noises in the middle of the night. If something makes a noise in the middle of the night it startles me and wakes me up so I know that I can hear while I'm asleep, and so the next secret was discovered. This is a Powerful secret.

Recite your mantra into a recorder and set it to play and repeat at night as you sleep. As you fall asleep, say the words of your mantra over and over again, but even after you fall asleep, your ears will hear the words and those words will be programmed into your subconscious Mind.

You will feel Powerful results. You will wake up the next morning and you will know that you have been programming yourself. You will know that you have gotten better even though you were sleeping. You will wake up feeling like a man or woman on a mission. You will have a sense of purpose and a sense of passion about the day you are about to take on.

If reciting and hearing your mantra becomes monotonous and boring, it's a good thing. That means that you are really chanting that mantra of yours. I never said it was going to be easy and fun all the time, but often the best things in life require sacrifice and discipline. Instead of watching TV as much, you will be studying books on the field in which you seek success. Instead of spending so much time on Facebook and Twitter like you used to, you will be surfing the Internet looking for tips and clues that will help propel you towards your goal. Instead of listening to the radio and your iPod that is filled with negative-energy music, you will be listening to your mantra on repeat, embedding what you desire for your life into your subconscious.

Sometimes you'll feel like taking a little break from it all and that's ok. If you feel like you need to just listen to some good ol' music, then by all means do it! If you do, I recommend that you create a mix CD or playlist that contains only inspirational, positive and uplifting songs. Once you Mind Cleanse and you start reprogramming your impressionable mind, you must be very careful about what you allow to creep into your fresh new mental computer. If you're curious, one of my favorite songs is "Closer", by Goapele.

WE
CONFORM

We are Conduits of Knowledge & Information

I believe what Dusty Baker believes. The baseball great spoke to the football team when I was at Stanford and he said:

None of us have ever achieved anything on our own. We have accomplished nothing in and of ourselves. If we think we have, we are foolish.

Dusty Baker is a former Major League Baseball player and current MLB manager. He was a two-time All-Star as a player and a World Series champion. He has won the National League Manager of the Year award three times.

We are not the originators of anything. There is nothing that will ever exist in this world that has not already existed in some form or fashion. Even when the light bulb was first introduced, it was operating on laws of the universe that had already existed. And the first steam powered locomotive was simply a different way of utilizing the laws of combustion that have always been in existence.

Don't believe me? I can prove it. Right now, try to come up with something in your mind that has never been thought of before. Try to create something that has never before been created, but I'm telling you that even the most wild, ridiculous and seemingly original creation that you can imagine will have components of things that have always existed. For example, a purple and yellow, polka-dotted, three-toed unicorn wearing military boots and sunglasses, although quite interesting, is made up of things that we already know. Even if we were to discover that this "completely new" species actually existed, we would realize that all of its individual parts have always been around; they were just pieced together in a new way.

That being said, anything that we will ever do or accomplish, is not completely original. We will never think of anything or do anything that hasn't already been done in some form or fashion. Think about it. Albeit a unique and highly individualized conglomeration, all that you are right now is a conglomeration of all that you have learned or experienced up until this point in your life. Although each of us is one-of-a-kind, we have become who we are based upon the things we have learned from other people and the specific experiences we have had. We have constructed thoughts, philosophies and concepts together in a unique way, building ourselves into the person we are now. Although the piecing together of knowledge and information has created the completely unique individual that we are, the parts of the sum have been passed down to us.

I know that I have not become who I am today all by myself. Others have helped shape and mold me into the person that I am today. I am a little bit of my family. I am my family. I know that I possess some of the qualities of my trainers, coaches and mentors. I know that I have also become who I am today by learning from my friends. I am my friends. The saying that we are born alone into the world and we die alone is just simply not true.

We have had mothers, fathers, brothers, sisters, teachers, coaches, friends, enemies and even complete strangers who have helped teach us and mold us into the people we are today. We should be thankful for all of the people and situations that we've encountered because they have helped us grow and develop. This is part of the circle of life. We learn, we grow and we pass on. However, we must not keep to ourselves all the life lessons we have learned. We must share what we know so that others, too, may benefit from our experiences. What a shame it is for one to die with all of their knowledge and experiences still trapped inside of them. What we have is not for us to possess, it is for us to pass on.

Again, the purpose of this book is to pass on to you some of that which I know has helped me thus far in my life. If I can pass along one piece of information or one thought that will resonate with you and make your life better, then the time it has taken me to write this book will have been worth it.

Surround YourSelf with Brilliance

It is very important to choose wisely the company you keep. It is human nature to conform to that with which we surround our-selves. Have you ever noticed that if someone in a group of people yawns, often at least one other person will yawn? Have you ever hung out with someone who curses a lot, and even if you don't say curse words you suddenly find yourself blurting out a four-letter word (or at least trying really hard to hold one back)? Maybe you've noticed that when two people are speaking to one another they will often mimic each other's body language? For example, if one person is standing with their hands on their hips, the other will eventually do the same. Next time you are talking to someone at a bar or get-together, try reaching out your hand and leaning on the bar or countertop while you talk to them. I bet you they do it too. Or, try putting your hands in your pockets or on your hips. Try crossing your arms or leaning up against the wall and watch what happens. The person across from you will eventually do the same. It's quite fascinating. We humans are funny, quirky creatures.

COY WIRE • WWW.COYWIRE.COM

If you often walk and talk with ducks, prepare to waddle and quack. Your friends will either uplift and inspire you or hold you back. Remember in high school all the different cliques? You had the cool crowd, the punk crowd, the jocks, the snooty crowd and the dorky crew to name a few. You could find these definitive cliques walking down the hallway or sitting at the lunch tables together. They would find comfort in being surrounded by others who wore the same types of clothing, had the same hair style, the same IQ level or the same type of humor. Even now and even more entertaining is that as adults these birds of a feather still flock together. It's amusing that adults are still doing it! Instead of high school cliques, they are now bar-scene cliques. Monkey see, monkey do. That's just how humans are.

Is it good to surround yourself with like-minded individuals who have the same morals and philosophies that you have? Yes. Whether they are acquaintances or co-workers, is it good to learn from positive people with whom we surround ourselves? Yes. However, we must beware of the wolf in sheep's clothing. Not everyone out there can be trusted. I know that there are certain people I have come across in life that I have had to stay away from. I knew that if I continued hanging around them I would develop bad habits and flawed character traits. How do you tell if a person is good or bad for you? A person's character can be judged by their actions. Do not go by what others say, go by what they do. A tree is determined by its fruit.

Beware of false prophets, who come to you in sheep's clothing but inwardly are ravenous wolves. You will know them by their fruits. Are grapes gathered from thorns, or figs from thistles? So, every sound tree bears good fruit, but the bad tree bears evil fruit. A sound tree cannot bear evil fruit, nor can a bad tree bear good fruit. Every tree that does not bear good fruit is cut down and thrown into the fire.

-Matthew 7:15-19

If a person produces good fruits, they are a keeper. If they are producing bad fruits, see ya later alligator. You may be able to be around them for a short time, but eventually it will get you.

I remember one time when I was young, my dog Boomer jumped into a very dirty and nasty pond. It was that type of pond where you look at it and say, "Man! That water must be contaminated with something!" He was having so much fun splashing through the water, but I knew that if I didn't get him out, something harmful might get to him. It just wasn't a healthy environment for him to be in and I was right. After I made Boomer get out, despite the fact that he was having so much fun and wanted to continue playing, I saw that Boomer had gotten leeches. These nasty little creatures had clung to Boomer and had begun to use him and feast upon him. I had to remove them immediately or Boomer would get sick and, literally, have the life sucked right out of him.

Our lives are like that of Boomer's. If we don't remove the leeches or any sort of negative influences from our life, they will make us weak and suck the life right out of us. Sometimes, people appear in your life as leeches. When they come into your life, you have to get rid of them as quickly as possible. Learn to swim in waters that are clean, clear, pure and beneficial to your growth and development.

There have been studies that show how people in social situations will conform to whatever the group does. Nobody wants to be the pariah. Most people want to "fit in", so they will go with the crowd so as not to stand out. Knowing this, we must choose wisely the company we keep. If we are forced to be in the presence of others we wouldn't necessarily choose to hang around, then we must be strong enough not to give in and act the fool.

My philosophy is simple: Hang around GOoD people who won't force you to be someone you don't want to be.

Remember that We conform to that with which We surround ourSelves.

Surround yourSelf with GOoD people

Now that we realize we conform to what we surround ourselves with, we should also realize that we need to choose our friends wisely. We need to be surrounded with uplifting people who have a positive attitude. Nobody can do this better than my wife and best friend, Claire. I chose to marry her because I knew that I would be committing myself for a lifetime to the opportunity of being around someone who is positive Energy, someone that can invigorate me and help me keep my Light shining brightly.

The more people you have in your life that can uplift you and bring positivity the better. I have made a pointed effort to surround myself with people who will enrich my life. So, why do I say you must get a "Roll" Model? What I mean is that you must surround yourself with friends like Michael Cassidy. Let me tell you about Mikey.

Have you ever noticed that many people who are physically "different" than others usually have the most tremendous outlook on life? You would think that people who have seemingly been dealt a short hand would see the world in a negative light. I mean, after all, they have every reason to have a crappy attitude, right? Usually that's not the case. I have met numerous people who, according to others, have physical "dis-abilities", yet they have outstanding mental and spiritual abilities. It seems as though when someone is not consumed by vanity and pride in their physical appearance, they are forced to focus on building the mental and spiritual aspects of themselves. They primp their personality, not their physicality. They build wonderful personalities and character.

Have you ever noticed how a blind person has a heightened sense of hearing because they depend on it more? Have you ever noticed how a deaf person has a heightened sense of sight because they exercise it more? Some of my closest friends have the best personalities and attitudes because they work on them.

I'm blessed to have Mikey in my life; he's an example of a GOoD person. He has been one of the most inspirational people I've ever encountered since I first met him and he is one of my very best friends. One of the things that makes Mikey unique is that he was born with cerebral palsy. What makes him even more unique is the infectiously positive attitude he maintains despite all the challenges he faces on a daily basis due to cerebral palsy. Because palsy has attacked his nervous system his muscles don't function properly, especially those in his lower body, forcing him to live his life in a wheel chair. It also impairs the dexterity in his hands slightly. The only sport Mikey could play was basketball in a wheelchair league. He could never play football or basketball the way most kids can growing up.

Mikey inspired me. His passion and zest for the game which he so badly wished he could play the way the rest of us could, helped him maintain a positive attitude no matter what, even though he seemingly had every reason to complain about the cards he had been dealt. In fact, Mikey will be the first to tell you that he has found cerebral palsy to be his greatest blessing. I often wondered whether I could have ever been as positive and happy as Mikey had I been born with cerebral palsy. What if I had to deal with all of the challenges, hardships and obstacles that Mikey did? Mikey is so strong in Mind and Spirit, whether he knows it or not, that I am forever grateful for the lessons he has taught me.

If Mikey was happy, thankful and grateful for the cards he had been dealt, then I better be able to remain grateful for all that I had. If, no matter what, Mikey can work to make others around him feel love and happiness, then I could too. If Mikey was able to build his character, Mind and Spirit, then I could too.

Each of us needs to have people in our lives that are positive motivating forces. Mikey always says, "Nobody should ever feel sorry for me. Being in a chair is God's purpose for my life and I've been blessed wonderfully!"

Mikey always says that his life couldn't be any better. He always gets parking spots in the front row. He is happy that he has been seated in a wheel chair his entire life because he is actually really short (4'11" to be exact), but now nobody will ever know!

As humans, we conform to what we surround ourselves with, so surround yourself with GOoD people. When you meet people in life who are positive and uplifting, be thankful. Cherish them for the positive influence that they are in your life. When someone like Mikey rolls into your life, you'll know it. When someone like Mikey rolls into your life, be thankful for that blessing.

MIND OVER MATTER

The Spiritual Movement

There is a movement that is happening in our country. This new movement is growing stronger every day thanks to people like you.

We are talking about the spiritual movement. There are many miracle workers in our country today who are creating positive change in the lives of others and doing great things to enable this spiritual movement to happen. There is a new awareness building in our world; a new consciousness that is growing in the hearts and minds of awakened beings in our world. It is the awareness and cognizance that what we think, say and do affects the world in which we live. It's a movement of Thought Manifestation.

The basics of the movement is the idea that what we think, say and do affects the world we live in and it is real. The Mind is everything. Physicists are now proving that our thoughts are actually energy.

Einstein said that energy can be neither lost nor destroyed. If that is true, then that would mean that our thoughts, which are Energy, cannot be lost or destroyed! That means thoughts live on forever.

Not only are our thoughts energy, they also manifest and become physical matter. Wise men from thousands of years ago knew this secret. They said:

Faith is the substance of things hoped for...

–Hebrews 11:1

Faith is a belief or thought, right? If that thought is a substance then that means a thought is an actual thing, a real and tangible object. You may say, "Wait, but, I can't see a thought." Well, you can't see air or electricity either, but there's no question those things are present. We know these things are made of physical mass that have tremendously powerful capabilities. Just because you can't see something doesn't mean it isn't real. We may not be able to see our thoughts but we can see the results of their existence. Our thoughts are Energy! How cool is that? And it's a powerful energy too.

Now hang with me here and try to follow this. If our thoughts are energy, or matter, that can be neither lost nor destroyed, then doesn't that mean that what we think and what we do now will live on forever? By that logic, our thoughts cannot be lost or destroyed.

Knowing this, imagine how powerful our thoughts are. I'm tired of people thinking carelessly and using thoughts carelessly. Speaking words (which are thoughts expressed) without realizing the power they possess. Thoughts and words have the ability to make or break someone's world, including your own. Do you know how powerful you are? Imagine the impact that your thoughts/energy/words have on this world? Imagine the impact of a positive thought or comment towards a child in need or a positive compliment to a friend at the right time. The things we think, say and do daily are never lost, they will be passed on. Even after we pass away, our Spirit will be passed on to and through those whose lives we've touched.

That's what is so exciting about this spiritual movement. It's exciting because you realize that your thoughts and words immortalize you. They allow the essence of Your Spirit to live on, in and through our youth and our future. Your thoughts and words will be your legacy allowing you to live on in our world forever because others will then pass on what they've received from you. This positive movement and your good works breathe new life and energy into all who are touched by the Energy and positive vibes that you have set into motion.

What we have said and done to others will be carried with them, will affect them and will in turn affect the things they think, say and do towards others. This will go on and on, affecting an unfathomable number of people. This cycle is never-ending. Down the line of time, from the lips of the queens and chambers of kings, through the writings and words of the sages, philosophers, mages, mothers, fathers, brothers, sisters and acquaintances, messages and thoughts have been passed down to us in this time and place. We now take what we have learned and pass down our thoughts and our actions that will also live on and affect the entire world and the future of our world. You are more powerful than you know.

There is proof of this. Look at all the great leaders of the past who have lived in our world and realized the power of their energy, thoughts and words. There are many children of the Light whose spirit still lives on today; whose thoughts and Energy live on today. The carpenter from a little town called Bethlehem, a mother named Theresa, a doctor named Martin Luther; all of their spirits live on and are kept alive to this very day.

Your Spirit, too, will live on and it will affect the world in which we live. It may not be as noticeable as some of the great men and women I've just mentioned, but do believe that you will have a great impact in your world.

You affect hundreds of people every day with your thoughts, words and actions. You affect your friends, cousins, brothers, sisters, colleagues, children and strangers. You are more powerful than you know. Nod your head if you've ever encouraged a kid who needed encouragement. Nod if you've ever held the hand of a timid child. Nod if you've ever brought a smile to someone's face simply by telling them they look nice today. As cliché as it is, keep nodding if you've ever helped an old lady cross the street or carried something heavy for someone who needed help. Keep nodding because you are more powerful than you know!

As you continue in your days and as this spiritual movement progresses, realize that you are the one that is affecting the world around you, and that collectively, we, are the ones shaping and building the lives of those around us and the future of the world in which we live. Yes, "we", not the governments, the media or the hierarchical powers that be, but we are the ones who decide every day what our future will hold. Every day, with every interac-

COY WIRE • WWW.COYWIRE.COM

tion, every conversation, every action and every thought, word and deed, you are building your legacy and expressing the Spirit of You that will be passed down through time and space and live on, forever. Hopefully you're still nodding your head because you're realizing that you are more powerful than you know.

While training in southern California with Marv Marinovich and Troy Polamalu, I learned many things about the potential we possess in the human body and, more importantly, in the human mind. Marv was extremely well-educated about the human body and its capabilities from a physical standpoint. Not only had he played professional football himself, Marv was one of the NFL's first strength and conditioning directors. He has trained hundreds of world-class athletes as he is now a full-time sports performance trainer. More than the physical aspect of training, though, Marv began to realize the importance of training the human mind. He has been fortunate enough to come across highly successful individuals who are among the world's best at what they do, and he has realized that they all have one thing in common: a powerful Mind.

I remember Marv telling us about a martial artist who is revered as one of the most dangerous men on the planet. For the purposes of this story we will call him SoulChild. Fighters came from all over the world to try their hand at this warrior. SoulChild does not fight in the public arenas. You will never see him on pay-per-view, or in the UFC. SoulChild is above those avenues of fighting. It is not about sport or entertainment for him. It is more like the underground fighting in the movie "Fight Club". This man fights for respect and honor. This spiritual warrior has trained his mind so well that he doesn't even have to touch people to defeat them. Marv told the story of how one particular time there was a martial arts master from The Orient who heard about the skills of SoulChild. The master from The Orient was actually a master of eight different disciplines of the martial arts. He took the long flight from overseas to the United States so that a match between him and SoulChild could be arranged. The two were to meet at a tiny building in the middle of the southern California desserts. It was on.

Troy Polamalu is a current NFL safety for the Pittsburgh Steelers. He's regarded as one of the best players in the NFL, a seven-time Pro Bowler and 2010's NFL Defensive Player of the Year.

A friend of Marv's who knows SoulChild was the one who drove SoulChild to the fight that night. They arrived late and everyone else was already there, inside and waiting. Marv's friend was getting ready to shut the car off and accompany SoulChild inside, but as he reached for the key, SoulChild stopped him and told him to stay in the car and to leave it running because what he came to do would be over in seconds, and they would be leaving in a matter of moments. Marv's friend did what he said. SoulChild went inside and just two minutes later he reemerged and said that it was time to leave. Marv's friend was somewhat shocked and later decided to find out what happened.

He was able to meet up with people from the fight later that night. He wanted to know exactly what had happened inside that building. One of the people discussing the occurrence had spoken to the master from The Orient who had just been defeated. As the group of men was sitting around a table reliving the event that had just happened, in a state of disbelief, Marv's friend learned what had occurred.

The master was waiting inside of a circle of onlookers for SoulChild to arrive. There was a buzz of energy going on around the underground fight club, murmurs of anticipation of what the outcome of these two legendary fighters' encounter would be. Finally, seemingly from nowhere, SoulChild quietly appeared through the crowd. He stepped into the ring, looked his opponent in the eye, bowed respectfully and walked toward the center of the ring. The master from The Orient bowed in return and also walked toward the center of the ring, but as he approached SoulChild, he suddenly stopped. It was almost as if he had run into an invisible wall and could no longer move any closer to SoulChild. SoulChild was just standing there, staring directly into the eyes of the master from The Orient. Then, bowing his head, the master from The Orient knelt down on one knee. SoulChild bowed respectfully and walked away. The fight was over.

When Marv's friend asked the other gentlemen what happened, they told him that the master from The Orient said that as he approached the center of the ring to fight, SoulChild froze him. They told him that SoulChild was using an ancient form of Tai Chi where a warrior uses energy, a spiritual sort of energy, to manipulate his opponent. SoulChild had so well trained his mind that he was able to use his mind to completely freeze and cripple his opponent so that he couldn't even move. The master from The Orient said that it felt like he had absolutely no strength, and that no matter how hard he tried, he couldn't move.

Everything Occurs in the Mind

Everything occurs in the Mind. Even all of the physical movements, recognitions and reactions occur in the mind. Eyes reflect
light and create images in our minds as thoughts. Sounds are
interpreted as vibrational patterns, wave lengths and frequencies
that produce thoughts and reactions in the Mind.

A huge mistake that most people make when they go to the
gym to train is that they go in thinking that they are going to train
their body. Wrong. That's why most people don't see the results
they want. If you are just going through the motions to train your
body physically at the gym by running, stepping, pushing or pulling, you will not get the results you want. Many people work and
work but never see major results because they still have a Mind
that hasn't been exercised. They still say things like, "I'm overweight. I need to lose a few. I will never look good." If this is your
Mindset, even with all the pushing, pulling, stepping and moving,
you're still losing.

When I go to the gym, I am not going in there to train my body. I am going to train my Mind. If you train your Mind, your body, your muscles and your physique will adapt. Wherever the Mind goes, the body will follow.

The Russians proved that our Mind wants to make everything equal. They proved that if you train with only your right arm, the left arm will grow bigger and stronger without even training it. Is it the body that is making the left arm grow stronger without even training it? No, of course not. It is the all-powerful Mind.

Every time I go for a workout session, I know that I am going to train by Mind, my body is just along for the ride. I am not building muscles, I am building confidence. I am not fine-tuning my body, I am fine-tuning my faith.

I go to the gym to get a mental workout. If I must do eight repetitions, I know that it is not my muscle that must lift the weight eight times. I know that it is my Mind that must conquer it and believe it because whatever I believe I can lift, my muscles will lift. Our bodies are capable of so much more than we give them credit for. You've all heard the story of the 80-year-old grandma lifting a car off of her grandchild.

If I have to do eight reps, 15 reps or 27 reps, my Mind must believe and conquer the challenge first or my muscles have no chance. My Mind must know that my body will get every rep. When I run sprints, I am not running to increase my physical endurance; I am running to grow my mental endurance.

With every rep, I have the opportunity to grow my ability to persevere. In a set of 15, 100-yard sprints, every single sprint is a challenge that my Mind must conquer, not just something that my body has to make it through. Remember, every time we work out every rep is an opportunity to strengthen our mind, the Mind that can do any and all things that will be used for GOoD. Go to every workout with the intention of getting a Mind training session, not a physical training session.

The power of the Mind is amazing. Your physical body is affected by the mental state you currently hold.

Several years ago, I was in Week 14 of the football season. I was feeling not only the mental strain of the season (monotony and discipline for a duration), but mostly the physical effects. My ankle, knee, lower back, shoulder, finger and neck were all crying out for me to stop the punishment. I noticed those body parts started to hurt even more when I found out that we weren't going to make the playoffs. Every morning getting out of bed it was painfully obvious that we had already played 13 regular season games, four preseason games and had endured a month of training camp. My body was hurting.

You know what the crazy thing is? After digging deep mentally and mustering up all the physical toughness and strength I could to battle through the last three games of the season, I was shocked at what happened after the final game of the season was over. As soon as I knew my body didn't have to endure any more beating something incredible happened. I woke up the next morning to find that almost all of my physical pains had disappeared.

Intuitively, sometime in the middle of the night while I was sleeping, my Mind realized that the season was over and it let out a big sigh of relief. The season was over. There was no more waking up at 5 a.m., weightlifting sessions, two-and-a-half hour practices and five hours of meetings. When my Mind relaxed, my body was relieved too. All the mental strain and stress was cumulatively straining my body. When my Mind went, "Ahhhhh", my body was also able to go, "Ahhhhhh." I was amazed. It wasn't my body that was hurting; it was my Mind that was beaten.

Not Too Loose, Not Too Tight

There is an old story about a musician who sought out the Buddha for guidance in practicing mediation. He asked, "How should I hold my mind when I practice? Should I try to concentrate hard and keep it under tight control, or should I relax and let it wander wherever it wants to go?"

The Buddha answered the musician with a question. "When you tune your instrument, do you make the strings too tight or too loose?"

The musician replied, "Neither too tight nor too loose. I make them just so."

The Buddha said, "In the same way as you tune the strings of your instrument, so you should hold your mind in meditation. Not too tight, not too loose, just so."

The Mind has the power to physically affect our bodies and we all know this. One of the leading causes of heart attacks is stress. Mental strain can trigger emotional problems such as insomnia, headaches and irritablitiy. Mental turmoil can play a part in problems such as high blood pressure, skin conditions and asthma.

A few years ago when Troy Polamalu suffered an injury in the middle of the football season, he said something to the media that baffled many. He was asked what he was going to do to help his body heal and recover quickly. Instead of saying that he would do special exercises and follow a strict rehabilitation regimen, he said he was simply going to lie on the couch and eat junk food. When asked why, he said that when his Mind was at ease, his body would relax and heal more quickly.

We must be able to find that happy balance with our state of Mind. Our attitude must not be one that is too lax and loose, or we will be like loose strings on an instrument that cannot make beautiful sounds. We cannot be too tight and stressed, or we will be like the instrument whose strings are strung so tight that they eventually snap.

When we are in pursuit of our passions we have to remember to enjoy life. We must not wind ourselves too tight that we eventually snap from the constant strain of going after our goals. Find a good balance in your life. Be disciplined but don't be destructively disciplined. Be focused but don't be foolishly focused. Keep peace of Mind by keeping it not too loose, not too tight.

PREPARE FOR
PORTALS
YOUR TIME IS
COMING

Patience - Become a Frog

You must believe that opportunity will come your way and that you will achieve what you desire.

People don't give frogs enough credit. I mean, they get such a bad rap. People tell lies about frogs, like they give you warts. The frog was ugly until the princess kissed it, removing the "curse", allowing it to become a prince. Ok, maybe it's true that they will pee all over you when you pick them up, but, I think frogs are brilliant and great teachers and an inspiration. Why? Frogs are trained killers. Frogs are carnivores. Frogs are meat eaters. Frogs are deadly predators. They eat flies and gnats and all kinds of other insects; what ruthless, stone-cold killers they are!

Especially impressive of the frog is that, unlike lesser species of carnivores like lions, tigers and cobras that have to expend all kinds of energy hunting down their prey and waste a lot of time thinking of the best strategy about when to attack, frogs don't have to do any of that. Frogs are the coolest killers on the planet. What makes them so lethal? Frogs get their prey using only one special weapon; a weapon that gets the job done every single time. Frogs use Faith.

Frogs are geniuses. They just sit on a lilly pad and wait. They chill there with monk-like patience and discipline, with the faith of a Saint, knowing that its meal will without question come to him. He doesn't have to hunt, he just sits patiently on the lilly pad, waiting. And when that insect inevitably flies past, the frog sticks out its tongue with cat-like quickness and snags it with little effort. Now that is faith, just sitting back waiting and knowing that your blessing will come. It doesn't know when, how or why, it just knows.

The true genius of the frog lies in its faith and patience. Is it no coincidence, then, that F.R.O.G. stands for "Fully Rely On God"? Hopefully you look at frogs differently now. They are wonderful creatures, creatures to be admired and studied. Frogs can teach us so much. We must become more like them.

We must be patient and have faith when we are waiting for our blessings to come; when we are waiting for our thoughts to manifest into physical reality. It takes time for our thoughts to become things; for the outside world that we see to align with the visual images we hold in our minds.

Some things may take years or even lifetimes to manifest, and other things may manifest instantaneously. The key is having faith that what we desire will manifest and the patience to wait for it to come. Like the Indian Guru Dattatreya Siva Baba says, "It is very important to know that usually a huge amount of time is needed for thoughts to manifest into visible reality. It's something like when you want to make ice cubes you have to put [water] in the freezer. The water then condenses into [solid] matter."

218

You must learn to open your mind and be ready to receive your gifts and blessings even when it begins to seem like they may not come. You must keep looking for them, listening for them and patiently waiting for them, because you do not know how, or when or why they will come, or by what means or manner. You only have to know that they will come! No one knows the hour or the day, only Your Subconcious knows. You must be ready at all times because when that fly flies past your lilly pad, you better be ready or you will not get the glory that is meant for you.

If you hope for something, you will always be hoping for it. If you wish for something, you will always be wishing for it. Conversely, if you know you have something, and if you are thankful that you already have it, then when that culminating point arises, that pivotal moment that is to determine whether or not you receive it, you will act and respond exactly the way you are supposed to, justifying your worthiness of it. All the mighty forces within you will come to your service. Whether you are a successful or not is determined by how you perform when the Door of Opportunity opens.

Preparation - Prepare for G.O.D. Doors of Opportunity.

It has been my observation that there will be a series of Defining Moments in life where you will have the opportunity to define yourself and advance yourself. How you perform in those "Defining Moments" will determine whether or not you reach your full potential in life. Each of these moments may only appear once and when they are gone, you may never get them back. When these Doors of Opportunity come to you, you must take full advantage of them.

I like to think of these "Defining Moments" as what I call G.O.D. Portals. In this scenario, G.O.D. stands for: Gaining One's Definition.

I learned that acronym from a poet and musical artist named Common. So, a G.O.D. Portal is a portal that opens for only a brief moment in time and space, and if you are able to recognize and seize that opportunity when it comes your way, you will be able to define yourSelf. You will become closer to achieving those things you have set out to achieve.

What determines whether or not one is prepared to take advantage of a Door of Opportunity when it comes? It all comes down to their faith in themselves. Do they believe in themselves? Do you believe? I am convinced that a person is able to believe in themselves when they know that they have done absolutely everything they possibly could have to prepare for the defining moment. If one has trained and prepared well, they will be ready; they can believe in themselves and their ability to get the job done. If, however, the person has not done everything they could have to prepare for the moment when it comes, there is no fooling themselves. One cannot trick themselves into believing. You can only lie to yourSelf for so long. The One within knows everything and sees everything.

Your prior mental training and programming determines whether or not you are worthy of passing through that Door of Opportunity when it opens. If you have prepared properly, using your MindTraining techniques, you will be worthy and ready when opportunity comes your way. You will be so well trained and prepared that you will run through that portal and your life situation will be accelerated by leaps and bounds closer to the proximity of your goal.

If you have not prepared properly for that defining moment, the Door of Opportunity will slam shut. No matter how hard you try, the opportunity to go through that door will have passed.

It is in your moment of decision that your destiny is shaped.

-Anthony Robbins

When opportunities present themselves to you, be sure that you are ready to seize them. This is where our Mind training comes into play. In the heat of battle, on the playing field or in the job interview, there will come one or several pivotal moments where our success or failure is determined by how we react or respond or act. They say in sports that it's a game of inches and the difference between success or failure happens in a fraction of a second. If you are prepared, you will act like a champion. Robert Collier likens this mindset to that of a cobra.

Think of a cobra that has spotted its prey and is coiled, ready to strike. It never once crosses the cobra's mind that it will miss its prey. We, too, must be so confident in our Self and in our training that it never once crosses our mind that we will fail. When opportunity comes our way, we will seize it violently.

The successful man sees an opportunity, seizes upon it, and moves upward another rung on the ladder of success. It never occurs to him that he may fail. He sees only the opportunity, he visions what he can do with it, and all the forces within and without him combine to help him win.

The unsuccessful man sees the same opportunity, he wishes that he could take advantage of it, but he is fearful that his ability or his money or his credit may not be equal to the task. He is like a timid bather, putting in one foot and then drawing it swiftly back again – and while he hesitates some bolder spirit dashes in and beats him to the goal.

-Robert Collier

Believe

Just because you set goals and plant seeds, does it mean that you will definitely receive the things for which you ask? Does it mean that you will definitely accomplish those goals? Will you automatically reap what you have sown? No. There is one more factor, another part to the equation that is as equally important as setting the goals and programming your mind for what you desire.

You will only receive as much as you believe you will receive.

If you do not have the confidence that you can do it, the faith that it will happen or if you feel that you do not deserve it, it won't happen!

You will only accomplish as many of your goals as you are able to imagine and believe in your mind that you will accomplish.

If you do not believe in your own abilities you will not be able to take advantage of Doors of Opportunity. As Orison Swett Marden says, "The way opens for the determined soul, the man of faith and courage.

It is the victorious mental attitude, the consciousness of power, the sense of mastership that does the big things in this world. If you don't have this attitude, if you lack self-confidence, begin now to cultivate it.

A highly magnetized piece of steel will attract and lift a piece of unmagnetized steel ten times its own weight. Demagnetize that same piece of steel and it will be powerless to attract or lift even a feather's weight.

The same difference exists between the man who is highly magnetized by a sublime faith in himself and the man who is demagnetized by his lack of faith, his doubts and his fears. If two men of equal ability, one magnetized by a driven self-confidence and the other demagnetized by fear and doubt, are given similar tasks, one will succeed and the other will fail."

Whether you think that you can or that you can't, you are usually right.

-Henry Ford

There's a difference in hoping for something and knowing you will get it. To be completely ready to take advantage of our opportunity when it presents itself, we must believe that we are ready to receive it. We can ask, but we must believe if we are ever going to be able to receive.

Belief comes from within. It comes from the confidence in knowing we are worthy of something. To believe in ourselves, we must know that we are worthy as a result of our proper training and thinking. If we are properly prepared, we will believe. If we believe, anything is possible.

Presence - Live in the Moment

When Doors of Opportunity present themselves we must be able to recognize and acknowledge them so that we can properly act upon them. Often, people never recognize their blessings when they come because they are caught in thought. They are not living in the moment so they don't actually see what is happening in the present moment. They are unable to see things for how they really are. We must be able to live in the moment, not the past or future, if we are going to be able to operate at a high level.

Everything that has ever happened in our past is somewhat of a figment of our imagination. Although the results, aftermath and memories of a past occurrence can still be present if we choose to keep it alive, specific past events no longer actually exist. Specific events from our past cannot affect us unless we, and those around us, allow them to. The past is dead.

Also, anything that will supposedly happen in our future does not exist (yet) and is merely a figment of the imagination as well. But, most people spend their entire day wondering about what

CHANGE YOUR MIND • PREPARE FOR PORTALS YOUR TIME IS COMING

they will do tomorrow. If they go out to meet up with their friends they wonder who might be there. Will it be fun? What will everyone be wearing?

Most people really are "out of their minds". They are not living in the here and now. Mentally, they are either somewhere out in the future or back in the past thinking about something other than what is going on right in front of them in the present moment. This causes them to only be partially effective and awake in the moment as it happens. We must learn to live in the now, with learnings from the past and planning constructively for the future.

People are not fully conscious for most of their lives. Technically they are awake, but they are day dreaming. They are dreaming about something that happened in the past or something that could happen in the future. So, they might as well be asleep, dreaming in their bed. Day dreaming prevents people from being completely awake and alive to the present moment. Much of their thought life is somewhere other than the present moment. Instead of having all of their mental capacity and focus in each moment as it is actually happening, they are day dreaming. A perfect example is when you are you are having a conversation with someone but they are text messaging on their cell phone at the same time. Did you ever notice that even though they are there with you and are talking with you, it's almost as if they are only half there? They are making sense and they are hearing you, but they are not really listening. I almost stole my young niece Lainey's cell phone last time Claire and I were back home because of how much she was texting while spending time with the rest of the family. I actually think there is a chance that she may not even remember us visiting and spending time with her! (She knows I still love her though.)

That is an extreme example, but an actually fairly accurate depiction of how most people go through their entire day thinking outside of the present moment. They may not be on a cell phone, but their mind is pre-occupied just the same. When you meet someone new, are you truly encountering that person completely? Or, as you shake their hand, are you thinking, "What's the deal with this person? They look weird. I know their type. Get me out of here." Suddenly you realize you were completely "zoned out" for the entire encounter and you can't even remember the person's name even though they just told you. You were "out of your mind". You were not in the present moment as it was occurring.

Nothing actually exists outside of this moment. Everything that ever happens in our world only happens in the present, the here and now. Anything that will ever happen will happen now. After this moment will be another and then another, but nothing ever happens any other time than right now.

One of the greatest assets of elite athletes and high-level performers is the ability to live in the moment. What does it mean to live in the moment? It means to be completely aware, focused and present in the here and now. There are no thoughts of future possibilities. There are no assumptions made about the present situation by comparing it to past experiences. The elite performers, artists and people in the business world are completely in tune with everything that is happening right now. For athletes it's called being in the zone.

As an athlete, being in the moment is crucial. Often in sport, the difference between a great performance and an average performance is a matter of milliseconds. That's a fraction of the amount of time it takes to blink an eye. That which separates the great athletes from all the others and the mighty from the mundane is the ability to be completely in the moment. When one is completely in the moment, they are able to be aware of every millisecond of the event that is happening around them.

If two athletes are going to race, and at the starting line athlete A is thinking about when his girlfriend is going to call him, while athlete B is completely in the moment, focused on the moment and listening for the gun to go off, who do you think will get the faster start when the gun goes off? Athlete B, of course, is going to get a head start and be milliseconds ahead of athlete A. Elite athletes know how to be in the moment at all times. They don't worry about anything or think of anything other than the here and now. The crowd doesn't faze them, the weather doesn't and being tired doesn't.

When the great artists and musicians create their most impressive works they are also in the zone, in a place of no-thought and only just creating. Incessant thinking does not get in their way. A vast majority of people spend 99 percent of their day living out of the moment. When in a situation, they are either thinking ahead about a mind-projected future or they are comparing the present situation to some past experience or situation.

The current situation and experience is completely unique and different from anything that has ever happened before so it deserves your undivided attention. When we live in the moment, we are able to take full advantage of every situation that Life presents us. We will not be a split-second behind when the moment of Truth comes, nor will we look back at a situation and wonder what if.

The grass is always greener syndrome is another example of living out of the moment. Do you have a friend that no matter where you go or what you do, they are never satisfied? If you go to a party, even if it's the best party of the year, they look around with a scoured face and talk about other things they could be doing. So if you take your friend somewhere else, before long they still want to seek out the next cool party or bar they just heard about. Instead of being able to enjoy the moment and enjoy the time and place where they are now, people who have "grass is always greener" syndrome are never satisfied because they are constantly thinking of something or somewhere else. If they could just become present, and stay focused on the present moment and soak up all that is going on around them right now they would realize that things aren't so bad and that your company, as their friend, is enough. They say that if you're the type of person who feels the grass is always greener somewhere else, then you're not taking care of your own lawn.

Live in the moment. Right here and right now is where all the Magic happens. Your true power performs optimally when you are completely in the present moment.

To be fully alive and thrive where you're at, see the world through the eyes of a cat

One way to practice living in the moment is by doing a little exercise that I call "Seeing the world through the eyes of a cat". I actually learned this from some random guy who came up to me and started telling me about the practice that his old karate master had him do. He walked up to me, seemingly overwhelmed with energy, and he started telling me how to see the world through the eyes of a cat. He talked quickly and pointedly, staring me directly in the eyes without wavering. He revealed this gift to me and then walked away, never to be seen again.

Cats are very good at living in the moment. They are much like the frog that sits upon the lily pad, breathing, taking life as it comes. Cats just sit and observe. They make no assumptions about any situation. They are not plotting or planning ahead saying, "What am I going to do next, or in an hour, or next week". Cats live in the moment. They don't plan ahead about when to eat, or think back about what they've eaten the past few days and worry if they've been eating too much. If they hear a loud noise, "BOOM", they are gone! That cat is out of there! They respond instantly to the situation because they are not caught in thought. They just react. This is the complete opposite of what most humans do. Remember the last time you watched a scary movie and you got so frustrated with the person in the movie because instead of just running out of the house when they heard the scary noise, they actually started thinking and went towards the killer and they died! Instead of just being in the moment, reacting to the situation by getting out of there like the cat would, they stayed, thought it through and they lost their life because of it. Let us not lose our lives to incessant thinking. Let us just live in the moment like cats do. Cats just live.

Seeing the world through the eyes of a cat is easy. You can do it anywhere. Put the book down for a second and look around. See the world, or room, or office, wherever you are, through the eyes of a cat. Make no judgments about what you see, don't think about anything you see, just observe. If you see a table, just notice the shape. Or if you look out the window, pay no particular attention to anything. Just observe. If you see a person, just notice the person. Do not make any judgments about what they are wearing or what they might do for a living or that they are ugly or good-looking. Just see them. Just see things...nothing more. When you are completely in the moment, like a cat, just seeing things as they are, without making any judgments or speculations, the things you see will actually appear different to you. You will notice things you've never really noticed before. Colors may be brighter. Textures may be more profound. You will really see things for the first time.

This exercise is particularly fun if you use it in a social situation, especially a bar scene. When you see the world through the eyes of a cat, you will really notice how weird and silly people are! They will look funny to you and the things they say will be, most of the time, meaningless and empty. You will wonder why people are acting the way they are. You will notice that many of them are drinking beverages even though they aren't thirsty. Cats must think we are really weird. Performing the cat exercise periodically will help teach you how to live in the moment, and when you get good at it, you will notice how your life will change for the better. It will become more meaningful and you will begin to appreciate and notice all the little things in life that you had been missing for all those years.

You will notice that your conversations with others become deeper, more meaningful and genuine. When you can see the world through the eyes of a cat others will sense this difference in your presence and awareness also. They will be attracted to you and drawn to your presence. You will be different than 99percent of the other people in this world. You will become one of those intriguing, interesting, cool people. Other's will say, "There's just something about that _____ (insert you name here)

ESSENTIAL STATES OF MIND

Gratitude.

We've learned that we must be thankful for the life we've been given, even for all the unpleasant situations we've had to endure. Good things come to those who remain positive through times of discomfort. Here's a story from my journals about a charmingly whimsical bathroom attendant I met one day in a bustling airport bathroom in Charlotte, NC. This man taught me a lesson about gratitude that day.

I started to walk through the little hallway, and it wasn't long before I realized that this visit to the bathroom was going to be more unique than any other I had experienced before. It was the most crowded bathroom I'd ever been in and I thought to myself, "Monday morning, lots of travelers."

Not only was the bathroom packed with people, but the air in the bathroom stunk with a festering funk of unpleasant aromas from said people. I walked in, turned the corner to walk down the row of "offices" and BAM! There he was right in my face saying "Good morning young fella!"

"Good morning" was my reply to the overly happy bathroom

attendant and I continued on towards my destination.

"Wow," I thought to myself, "that's a happy old fella." The bathroom was so incredibly busy; I actually had to wait to use the facilities. As I was waiting I noticed that this old man's Energy and enthusiasm did not waver as he greeted every person who walked through the doorway and said "goodbye" as they left.

"Hello there, welcome to Charlotte!"

"You're in Charlotte, happy Monday!"

"Have a great week now sir!"

"Happy Monday to ya!"

"Good mornin to ya 'New York'," he said to the kid in the Yankees hat.

In and out people would walk. I must've heard him greet over 50 people and he had a big old smile on his face with every interaction. His big smile made me smile. His happiness gave me happiness.

I'd hear him say "Appreciate ya sir! Have a great day!" and I realized that others, like I was going to, were tipping this old man just because he was in there making them smile too.

As I walked to the sink to wash my hands I grabbed some money out of my pocket and then formulated my thoughts as I washed my hands. I just had to ask this old man how he could be so happy and kind despite his situation. I mean, like I said, the bathroom was packed, crowded, and it was early in the morning. People were grumpy on this Monday morning and the bathroom stunk real badly. He was in there wiping down counters smiling and picking up trash on the floor practically before it even landed.

I approached him, his eyes glistening and a smile on his face. We made eye contact and he nodded and said, "Have a great day young man."

I walked straight to him, leaned in and whispered (I was kind of embarrassed that I was going to interview the guy working in the bathroom), "How are you able to stay so happy?"

"What's that young man" he whispered back with a smile.

"How are you able to be so happy?"

He leaned back crinkling his brow, staring deep into my eyes, "Ooh I got to. I ain't got time to put up with other peoples' shit!"

I chuckled at the irony of the response. Here was this old man in a stuffy bathroom that smelled like crap, saying that he hasn't got the time to deal with peoples' crap! He was choosing to be positive and not let negative people or circumstances get to him!

"Life's too short," he said. "We have to be thankful for what we have. We can create our own heaven and our own hell right here on Earth."

I was smiling nodding my head in agreement. I smiled and said that I believe that too. He smiled, nodded back and told me to have a great day. I gave him a tip and walked away.

My tip paled infinitely in comparison to the tip he gave me that day. He reminded me of the valuable lesson that it's not what happens to us, it's how we go through it. We see the world not as it is, but how we are on the inside. Life is too short to let crappy situations stink up our days. Life is too short to let crappy people be party poopers in our days. We have to be thankful for each and every moment. If life hands you lemons, make lemonade.

If you want to be happy, be.

-Leo Tolstoy

When you wake up, stretching and yawning, set your day up, set the tone in the morning

Okay, well maybe not literally but here is something that I want you to try. It's helped me from time to time over the years, especially during those times when it was just "one of those times". When you sense it is going to be "one of those days", you have to jump out of bed in the morning as if it were on fire. Okay maybe not literally jump out of bed, but sit up and stand up quickly! Mentally, you must get up and GO. You must shock your system. Use the law of inertia. Whatever you set the tempo to be first thing in the morning will be the tempo of the rest of your day. Use this trick when you are feeling sluggish when that alarm goes off. (Hopefully, you didn't just say to yourself, "that's every day"

When you set the mental tone for your day, your vibe is set for the whole day. There will probably be mornings when you are

CHANGE YOUR MIND • ESSENTIAL STATES OF MIND

tired and "dread" the day before it even gets started, but show your body and your brain that You are the Captain of this vessel and that You have already made the decision it is going to be a WONDERFUL day!

What little kid wakes up on the day of his birthday with a crappy attitude? Even though that day is really just a day like all the others, the kid wakes up happy and excited for the day! The kid knows that people are going to be nice to them and they are going to be given gifts so they are ecstatic and can't wait to jump out of bed to get the day started. Well, buddy, guess what. Each of your days is filled with gifts too. Each day offers many gifts and opportunities that we can be excited about.

What kids wake up on Saturday morning and say, "I don't wanna go play with my friends or watch Saturday morning cartoons"? And what about Christmas morning? How many little Christian kids wake up on Christmas morning mad? Why is it that the child is going to get up out of bed excited in the morning...getting up out of bed looking forward to the day that lies ahead? It's because they are looking forward to what they know is going to be a great day. That is what we must do every day, and it's much easier to do when we have goals that we are excited about, that we know we will achieve...we know that each day brings us one step closer to that which we desire. Have positive expectations for each and every day. Set the tone in the morning. Set your bed on fire.

Stay Positive: Become an Alchemist

As meriam-webster states:

Alchemist: a person who studies or practices alchemy.

Alchemy: 1 : a medieval chemical science and speculative philosophy aiming to achieve the transmutation of the base metals into gold 2 : a power or process of transforming something common into something special 3 : an inexplicable or mysterious transmuting

Change the world aroud you by changing the way you see it.

A true story by Dr. Charles

Dr. Charles Garfield is an American writer and motivational speaker. He is considered one of the country's leading minds on achievement. As a computer scientist, he was part of the team of engineers that put Apollo 11 on the moon, a project that helped him discover his principles on peak human performance.

Garfield sums it up best...here's a version of that story.

If you have ever gone through a toll booth, you know that your relationship to the person in the booth is not the most intimate you'll ever have. It is one of life's frequent non-encounters: You hand over some money; you might get change; you drive off. I have been through every one of the 17 toll booths on the Oakland-San Francisco Bay Bridge on thousands of occasions, and never had an exchange worth remembering with anybody.

Late one morning in 1984, headed for lunch in San Francisco, I drove toward one of the booths. I heard loud music. It sounded like a house party, or a Black Eyed Peas concert. I looked around. No other cars with their windows open. No sound trucks. I looked at the toll booth. Inside it, the man was dancing.

"What are you doing?" I asked.

"I'm having a party," he said.

"What about the rest of these people?" I looked over at other booths; nothing moving there.

"They're not invited."

I had a dozen other questions for him, but somebody in a big hurry to get somewhere started punching his horn behind me and I drove off. But I made a note to myself: Find this guy again. There's something in his eye that says there's magic in his toll booth.

Months later I did find him again, still with the loud music, still having a party.

Again I asked, "What are you doing?

He said, "I remember you from the last time. I'm still dancing. I'm having the same party."

I said, "Look. What about the rest of the people."

He said, "Stop. What do those look like to you?" He pointed down the row of toll booths.

I said, "They look like toll booths."

He said, " Brother, you've got noooo imagination!"

I said, "Okay, I give up. What do they look like to you?"

He said, "Vertical coffins."

"What are you talking about?"

"I can prove it. At 8:30 every morning, live people get in. Then they die for eight hours. At 4:30, like Lazarus from the dead, they reemerge and go home. For eight hours, brain is on hold, dead on the job, going through the motions."

I was amazed. This guy had developed a philosophy, a mythology about his job. I could not help asking the next question:

"Why is it different for you? You're having a good time."

He looked at me.

"I knew you were going to ask that," he said. "I'm going to be a

245

dancer someday."

He pointed to the administration building.

"My bosses are in there, and they're paying for my training."

Sixteen people dead on the job and the seventeenth in precisely the same situation, figures out a way to live. That man was having a party where you and I would probably not last three days. The boredom! He and I did have lunch later, and he said, "I don't understand why anybody would think my job is boring. I have a corner office, glass on all sides. I can see the Golden Gate, San Francisco, the Berkeley hills; half the Western world vacations here and I just stroll in every day and practice dancing.

Become an Alchemist and turn base metals into gold, transforming something common into something special. Inexplicably and mysteriously transform seemingly negative situations into positive ones.

Let us rise up and be thankful, for if we didn't learn a lot today, at least we learned a little, and if we didn't learn a little, at least we didn't get sick, and if we got sick, at least we didn't die; so, let us all be thankful.

— Siddharta Gautama

Abraham Lincoln said, "Most people are about as happy as they make up their minds to be." I would tend to agree with that. If life hands you lemons, make lemonade. If life is corny, make popcorn. If parts of your life are crappy, flush them down the toilet.

Everything that you are, and your perception of all that you have done is a direct result of the state of Mind you've had. All of the accomplishments and failures you've had were influenced by your state of Mind. All of the happiness and sorrow you've felt were a reflection of your state of Mind. All of the peace and regret that you've experienced were because of your state of Mind. Your state of Mind has been affecting the outcome of your life ever since your were able to make rational decisions. Not only has it shaped your life up until this moment, but your state of Mind will shape your future too.

If you want to take control of your life, you must take control of your Mind.

Perseverance

Through football and the challenges it presents I've learned so much about the human mind, about faith and about belief. I've learned that we are all more powerful than we know.

Checkout the story I did on my YouTube page:

http://www.youtube.com/user/CoyWireDotCom

We will all face adversity in our lives. We need adversity in our lives to put us in a place of discomfort. Sometimes we live our lives too comfortably, going through the motions and the monotony of the day keeps us in a stagnant place. When we are faced with adversity, whether it is injury or trauma of emotional, physical, mental or relational nature, it forces us to re-examine our current life situation. It may show us that there may be things that we need to change in our lives so that we do not continue to remain stagnant and trapped in the vicious cycle of mediocrity.

248

Adverse situations often force us to grow stronger in a positive direction so that we no longer stay stagnant. We are forced to
overcome the mundane and monotonous life that we were living;
the under-achieving life with which we were content. Adverse
situations force change and as long as you keep a positive attitude
and are willing to see the potential for growth going through that
adversity you will become a Victor through that situation and not a
victim.

You must keep a positive state of mind so that you can persevere towards greatness as opposed to crumble and cower to an
imprisoned place of arrested development. You must maintain the
Mind of a Champion. How you go through adversity mentally will
determine how you come out of it. Always remember to embrace
adversity and see it as a challenge which forces you to grow
stronger and to become a better person. Become stronger, harder
and more ready for anything. The strongest steel is burned in the
hottest coals.

You will be put through the fire, you will be put to the test and
you will get burned and it may burn badly, but like that steel that
is burned and put through the smoldering flames, you too will be
refined and strengthened and become harder and harder because
of the fire. The same thing is true of diamonds.

The most precious and beautiful stone on the planet exists
because it was put through pressure and was constricted and
stressed. It originated as an ugly dirty piece of coal, but over time,
because of the compression and pressure and stress, it was made
beautiful. It was hardened, refined and made pure. Through adversity, an undesirable and ugly piece of coal is transformed into a

beautiful, valuable diamond. So embrace the struggle.

Learn to see the opportunity for growth through your trials and tribulations. See that your adversities make you more able to persevere and that they make you stronger than others who did not have to go through what you've been through. They didn't have to go through the same trials and tribulations you've had to over-come. They may have had their own but they may not ever be able to understand yours. So accept yours as a precious gift and as an exclusive opportunity that only you have received.

See your personal trials as revelations which point to the changes you need to make within yourself to be the best person you can be. Will you come out a Victor or a victim? The choice is yours. We must not shy away from obstacles in our life. In fact, we should embrace them. Whenever we are able to overcome obsta-cles we become stronger. Difficult times strengthen us and refine us. Our struggles force us to grow our perseverance.

Embrace your struggles.
They make you who you are.
There is no one in the world like you.

- Coy Wire

The following excerpt is from "The I Ching", an ancient book of Chinese wisdom.

CHIEN/DEVELOPMENT (GRADUAL PROGRESS)
Those who persevere make continuous progress.

The image of this hexagram is that of a tree growing high on a mountaintop. If this treed grows too fast, without first properly rooting itself, it becomes susceptible to being torn up and destroyed by the winds. If, however, it establishes a proper foundation and is content to grow gradually, it will enjoy a long life and a lofty view.

Human beings are no different. While we often desire rapid progress – we want to change someone's mind today, obtain an apology now, achieve all our goals immediately – sooner or later we must come to understand that the only lasting progress is gradual progress. Chien comes to urge you to accept that fact and base your thoughts, attitudes, and actions upon it.

This excerpt is taken from the Brian Browne Walker's translation of "The I Ching".

When we have allowed ourselves to be pulled off balance by another or by some event, the ego tempts us to believe that we can influence the situation through forceful

CHANGE YOUR MIND • ESSENTIAL STATES OF MIND

behavior. This is incorrect; the actions of the ego inevitably complicate our difficulties. The greatest influence possible always comes through the patient and steady refinement of one's inner self. If you will devote yourself to the path of the Sage, with every step along that path you will be strengthened, and progress will come automatically. It will be gradual, but it will last.

Be patient, modest, and accepting now. Life often demands that we wait longer than we might like for some change, and the only true comfort available during these times is the knowledge that we are steadfastly developing ourselves into superior people. In time, every honor comes to those who are persevering and correct.

10

BECOME A BOOKWORM & ACQUIRE KNOWLEDGE

Acquire Knowledge

If we want to continue to be the best that we can possibly be, we must never be satisfied and we must always be hungry for knowledge. Author Jon Gordon said that he was speaking at a seminar on self-improvement, and sitting in the front row taking notes was Zig Zigler. At 88 years old, one of the greatest motivational speakers of all time, Mr. Zigler was sitting in the front row taking notes and trying to make himself better.

Never be content. We live in a society that has made it acceptable to settle. Don't ever settle. Commit yourself, as Gordon says, to being a lifelong learner.

I see our youth today spending hours upon hours playing video games, texting and surfing the Internet. Those hours could be spent acquiring knowledge that will help them achieve their goals. If you want to be a professional video game player, then video games are a productive use of your time. However, if you're an athlete you could be reading books about great athletes and what made them better. If you're an aspiring business owner, you could be reading books about entrepreneurship. If you are an aspiring musician or artist you could take lessons or find a mentor. If you are a mother or father, you could read books about parenting or leadership.

People are becoming very lazy. People are becoming more and more like slugs that sit inside all day and waste away all of their talents and abilities on activities that get them nowhere in life. Have you ever gone to a local bar or restaurant in your hometown to find, sadly, the same people sitting at the same bar, drinking the same drink, smoking the same cigarette? Aside from being a little older and a little more overweight, nothing has changed in their life.

Most people don't realize that they are starving for knowledge. Most people don't realize that they crave knowledge. However, when that day comes and they get a whiff of what is out there for them to discover, they become ravenous. They become hungry for knowledge again, just like when they were children and they wanted to know the reason for everything. When one discovers that they can learn anything they need to learn in order to achieve their goals, they become eager to acquire knowledge pertaining to them. When one realizes that they need not sit back and wait for information to come to them, that they can go out and gather information for themselves, they become hungry. The more they learn, the more they realize that there are no limits to what they can do.

Seek and acquire knowledge that will provide you with the proper tools to work your way towards a wonderful life. We must always be hungry for knowledge. We must always seek to improve ourSelves so that we can maximize our full potential.

What is a bookworm? It is a living being that gets sustenance from eating the paper in books, ingesting all that is within. Yes, there are actually tiny critters that are book-borers. Most commonly it is referred to as a booklouse or paper louse. These book eaters use books to give them strength and sustenance. You must do the same. Eat books up. Gobble them one after another!

eats books to live; Read books, ingest and digest what's within

The last Secret that I can reveal to you is to do what you are doing right now: read. Always have a book on hand. It should be a book that is relevant to one or more of your goals; a book that deals with topics beneficial to you. It's a great way to keep your goals in your conscious mind. It's a great way to learn more methods to achieve your goals. Instead of wasting valuable life moments on television, video games, surfing the web or emailing, you should be soaking up information that will empower you. Do this as often as you can and acquire knowledge! (As long as you're not chanting your mantra!)

Read books that will help you get to where you want to go. Read every chance you get. Read first thing in the morning over coffee, read during lunch breaks, read while you're in the bathroom and read before bed. Read while driving. Well, sort of. I often have inspirational audio books for the car. Like Dr. Earl Suttle says, "Become a Road Scholar, your car can become the world's greatest library, you can be the greatest student enrolled at Mercedes University!"

The Roland Berger study showed that Americans average 540 hours per year in a car, twice as much as Europeans. We should be twice as knowledgeable as Europeans! Like a bookworm, eat books and constantly be feeding yourSelf knowledge and information that is pertinent to your purpose.

The heart of the prudent getteth knowledge; and the ear of the wise seeketh knowledge.
— Proverbs 18:15

11

TO BEE OR
NOT TO BEE

To Bee or Not To Bee

Think back to what it was like to be a child. Anything was possible. You believed in magic, possibility and fantasy. When you were young, you wanted to know the "whys" and the "hows" of things. You were a dreamer. You were hope-FULL. Anything and everything seemed possible. You probably didn't know the definition of "can't". You knew not of limitation or lack. You see, when we were children, unscathed by cynicism and age, the world was a magnificent setting for anything we wanted to accomplish or create.

When we were young we were imaginative, innovative and big dreamers. What were some of the things you used to do or believe in? How did you see the world before some party pooper came along and told you how you were supposed to see it? What types of possibilities existed in this world before you were forced to read textbooks in school that told you how to think, what was possible and what to believe? What did you believe was possible before your teacup was full?

You used to think differently and dream differently before all the party-poopin' began. As you got older, I'm sure you began to hear about all of the laws that exist, laws that told you what is possible and what is not. Somewhere along our paths, we were told that certain things are impossible, that we are unable to overcome particular feats, accomplish certain goals and that a portion of our dreams were frivolous. Even though you may have tried to resist at first, at some point you probably gave in and began to believe them. Our teacups became full.

Unfortunately, these ill-conceived "teachings" burst the bubbles we fostered when we were children, thus clouding our perceptions of what we really can accomplish and what we really should dream. If you heard enough people tell you something was not possible, you started to believe them and in believing them you gave up your hope and your belief in yourself. Eventually, your hopes became smaller, and your dreams meeker. Pretty soon you were walking around trained like everyone else. You were programmed how to think, you were told what to believe and you were trained as to what was possible and what was not. That's where the Magic was lost.

That's pretty sad, isn't it? I am sick and tired of these ignorant people who take away the pearls of children's wisdom. I know that if we were never told what we can't accomplish or shouldn't dream, we would be more powerful and successful than we can imagine. Unfortunately, through the process of maturing, we have slowly built up mental blocks against possibility. Just like a callous on our hands, we slowly but surely become insensitive to things around us.

For instance, there is a reason why people say that the majority of people who can see angels and spirits are children; it is because no has told them that they don't exist or that they can't see them. However, as we get older, we are told that angels and spirits are things of fairy tales and all of a sudden we are blind to them. The antithesis of this is found in the ability of the bumblebee.

According to the laws of aerodynamics, it is physically impossible for bumble bees to fly. Their bodies are too round and too heavy and their wings are neither strong enough nor beat fast enough to lift their bodies off the ground and fly them through the air.

So why is it that bumble bees can fly? Because nobody ever told the bumble bee it could not fly. They believe that they can fly. I'm convinced that if bumble bees had ears and were able to understand English and if people repeatedly told them they could not fly, we would soon have a new species of bee that walked around on the ground all day stinging people's feet. These underachieving bees would be grumpy and unfulfilled because they wouldn't be living the high-flying lives they were meant to live.

Fannie Lou Hamer was an American voting rights and civil rights activist and leader. She became the Vice-chair of the Mississippi Freedom Democratic Party.

I'm sick of all of the party poopers! I'm tired of hearing phrases like, "You'll never be able to do that." Like Fannie Lou Hamer said, "I'm sick and tired of being sick and tired." Too often people are telling us what we can and can not do.

What if nobody ever came along and told you how to think? What if party poopers never told you what is and is not possible? What if you were never told what you could or could not do? Would you have dreamed bigger? Would you have hoped for and aspired for more?

Let us be reborn mentally. Let us make a vow to ourSelves that we will stand strong in our beliefs and be dedicated to who we are. We must never let others tell us of what we are capable. We must never let anyone tell us what is and what is not possible. We must be more like the bumble bee who flies because it believes it can. We need to work on scraping away those calluses that have built up over the years. We must become more childlike in our thinking.

Let us revert back to a time when we were carefree, a time when we didn't care what other people thought. We must go back to the innocence of our youth when our thoughts were free and our hopes and dreams were untamed. We must go back before the time of our arrested development. We must go back to being innovative and creative with our thinking and be not afraid to dream big and huge dreams that make no sense to others. Remember what you have forgotten. You can do anything. You can BEE anything. Let us be born again.

And said, Verily I say unto you, Except ye be converted, and become as little children, ye shall not enter into the kingdom of heaven.

— Matthew 18:3

Chief Tecumseh's Words of Wisdom

So live your life that the fear of death can never enter your heart.

Trouble no one about their religion; respect others in their view, and demand that they respect yours.

Love your life, perfect your life, beautify all things in your life.

Seek to make your life long and its purpose in the service of your people.

Prepare a noble death song for the day when you go over the great divide.

Always give a word or a sign of salute when meeting or passing a friend, even a stranger, when in a lonely place.

Show respect to all people and grovel to none.

When you arise in the morning give thanks for the food and for the joy of living.

If you see no reason for giving thanks, the fault lies only in your-self.

Abuse no one and no thing, for abuse turns the wise ones to fools and robs the spirit of its vision.

When it comes your time to die, be not like those whose hearts are filled with the fear of death, so that when their time comes they weep and pray for a little more time to live their lives over again in a different way.

Sing your death song and die like a hero going home.

About the Author

Coy Wire is a Pennsylvania native who set his mind towards achieving his dream of playing football in the NFL at an early age. While focused on this goal he began to unlock the secrets in this book. He attained a Bachelor's Degree in Sociology and served as a team captain of the Stanford football team. From Stanford he was drafted into the NFL by the Buffalo Bills. After recovering from a life-threatening injury he joined the Atlanta Falcons where he finished his nine-year professional career. He has been a captain for every team he's played on since high school, and, more importantly has become a "captain" in the lives of many teenagers through his Mind Coaching services and community leadership.

Learn more about Coy and retraining your brain at
www.coywire.com